ADVANCE PRAISE FOR THE SACRED KITCHEN

For some the world is a garden to tend and for others it is a kitchen in which to prepare nourishment. Read the words of this book and nourish your body and soul and the world around you.

— Bernie Siegel, M.D.
author of *Love, Medicine & Miracles* and *Prescriptions for Living*

The Sacred Kitchen is a beautifully written guide to the power of foods for health. Its ideas are rooted in time-tested traditions, yet are refreshingly new. It is both thought provoking and eminently practical. I highly recommend it.

— Neal D. Barnard, M.D.
president, Physicians Committee for Responsible Medicine

The Sacred Kitchen is a wonderful anomaly in the realm of cookbooks — you can't put it down! The recipes are easy and delicious, and the writing makes us realize how important a part food plays in our homes. This book helps us organize our kitchens, our food, and our cooking in a way that brings a consciousness of sacred balance to our everyday lives.

— Vimala McClure
author of *A Woman's Guide to Tantra Yoga* and *The Ethics of Love*

When we eat, are we feeding just our bodies, or are we also nurturing our souls, and our connection to all of life? In *The Sacred Kitchen,* we learn how to bring health and harmony into every meal, and wholeness into every life. I highly recommend this important book.

— John Robbins
author of *Diet for a New America* and *The Awakened Heart*

Food is the offspring of the magical marriage of Heaven and Earth. As the materialization of pure love, it gives us life. To honor food is to honor the Creator. *The Sacred Kitchen* unifies this understanding in the spiritual hearts of all people and their life-protecting culinary traditions throughout the ages. *The Sacred Kitchen* nourishes the heart and soul of our own being. No one will go away hungry.

— Cecile Tovah Levin
author of *Cooking for Regeneration*

the sacred kitchen

the
sacred
kitchen

Higher-Consciousness Cooking for Health and Wholeness

Culinary Wisdom, Ancient Traditions,
and Vegetarian Recipes to Transform Your Life

ROBIN ROBERTSON and JON ROBERTSON

New World Library
Novato, California

New World Library
14 Pamaron Way
Novato, California 94949

The authors wish to express their gratitude to the following publishers and authors for permission to quote their work:

Excerpts from *The Path to Self-Healing: Sotaiho* © 1996 by Sensei Shigeru Kanai. Reprinted by kind permission of the publisher: Terra Bella Publishing, P. O. Box 3941, Virginia Beach, VA 23454.

Excerpt from the book *Diet for a New America* © 1987 by John Robbins. Reprinted by permission of H J Kramer, P.O. Box 1082, Tiburon, CA 94920. All rights reserved.

Quotations from *Taoist Secrets of Love: Cultivating Male Sexual Energy* © 1984 by Mantak Chia and Michael Winn (ISBN 0-943358-19-1). Reprinted by permission of Aurora Press, P.O. Box 573, Santa Fe, NM, 87504.

Excerpts from *The Golden Present* © 1987 and *Gems of Wisdom* © 1988 by Swami Satchidananda. Reprinted by permission of Integral Yoga® Publications, Satchidananda Ashram-Yogaville, Buckingham, VA 23921

The Great Invocation used by kind permission of The Lucis Trust, 120 Wall Street, 24th Floor, New York, NY 10005.

Quotations from *A Taste of Heaven: Adventures in Food and Faith* by Rabbi Lionel Blue and June Rose © 1977 are used by permission of Templegate Publishers, 302 E. Adams Street, P.O. Box 963, Springfield, IL 62705, and Darton, Longman & Todd, London.

Excerpts from *Cooking for Regeneration* © 1988 by Cecile Tovah Levin. Reprinted by permission of Cecile Tovah Levin.

Quotations from *Eco-Cuisine* © 1995 by Ron Pickarski. Reprinted by permission of Ten Speed Press, Berkeley, California.

Library of Congress Cataloging-in-Publication Data
Robertson, Robin (Robin G.)
   The sacred kitchen : higher consciousness cooking for health and
wholeness / by Robin & Jon Robertson.
              p.   cm.
      ISBN 1-57731-092-6 (alk. paper)
      1. Robertson, Jon.   II. Title.
      TX652,R637   1999
      641.5 — dc21   98-52992
                                                                              CIP

First Printing, April 1999
ISBN 1-57731-092-6
Printed in Canada on acid-free paper
Distributed to the trade by Publishers Group West

10 9 8 7 6 5 4

This book is dedicated to
those who seek the sacred in everyday life
and to those who cook with love.

CONTENTS

ACKNOWLEDGMENTS

The authors express their gratitude to the following people, whose assistance, encouragement, and contributions helped greatly in producing this book: Gina Misiroglu, Arielle Eckstut, Neal Barnard, M.D., Bernie S. Siegel, M.D., John Robbins, Vimala McClure, Cecile Tovah Levin, Danny Lliteras, Carole and James Lazur, Huizhen Zhang, Patty Gershanik, Cindy and Pete Kube, Lisa Lange, Judy Wicks, and Father John Giuliani.

INTRODUCTION

Food — God's love made edible. May we be swept into Your presence.
— Brother Thomas, the Nada Hermitage

Until the twentieth century, the hearth had always been the center of the home. It was the kitchen center around which the family kept warm, fed itself, and discussed the day's work. Father, mother, children, and grandparents knew each other's faces by firelight. Each member, even the children, had chores to do, important contributions to make every day that helped the family to survive. At day's end, family members gathered in the kitchen, preparing and eating their meals, praying, laughing, and planning.

The twentieth-century's legacy to the twenty-first is our loss of this archetype of hearth and home. Individual family members are no longer essential to the family's survival, outside of those who earn money. We rely on those who cook the meals, often eating prepackaged, processed, microwaveable food units in minutes flat. We attempt to tame the uncertainties of the new millennium, struggling for physical health while trying to ignore a deeper hunger for relevance and meaning.

The Sacred Kitchen hopes to help satisfy that hunger by rekindling the idea of the kitchen hearth. It will reveal the hidden energies and holy purposes that can revive the kitchen's central importance in the home. It is a practical guidebook meant to inspire family and friends alike to once again pull together for their physical, mental, and spiritual nourishment, particularly at mealtimes. Equally important are its recipes and cooking techniques for creating excellent, healthy, vegetarian meals in what is to become the stress-free holy place of your kitchen.

This approach to restoring physical and spiritual health is the result of our studies and experience, but also of our personal effort to overcome pressures that had at one time mounted beyond our control. Earning a living had driven us into different schedules, in which sit-down meals had been replaced by eating on the run. Intimacy and conversation between us had dwindled to nothing.

It was during the late 1980s when we realized that our lives and relationship were in danger not as in the days of old when a crop failure could doom the family, but simply due to the stress of trying to match our creative abilities with a dwindling job market and losing our health from poor dietary habits and limiting attitudes.

Married for seventeen years, we were living in beautiful Charleston, South Carolina, Jon working as a freelance writer and Robin as a chef in the busy restaurant trade. We had both been students of religious and metaphysical thought since the 1960s. But despite our previous studies and spiritual practices, we were working and playing too hard to pay attention to the practical matters of spirit: talking to God and feeling connected to the Divine.

Robin had spent eight years in restaurant kitchens, working her way up from line cook to chef. Her life dream had turned into endless hours of staggering responsibilities. Those hectic sixteen-hour workdays were filled with nonstop stress and unrelenting demands on her body, mind, and spirit. It took a heavy toll on our relationship, as well. That was why she eventually quit the restaurant business — even though she didn't know what she would do next. Together, we decided to make ourselves healthy again and try to rediscover our sense of purpose in the universe.

We began studying and reading together for the first time in years. Robin concentrated on books about diet, nutrition, and cooking, while Jon focused on philosophical subjects. We had begun to undergo a spiritual reawakening: getting back in touch with what was important in life. Robin began to experiment with healthier eating, and cooking together became one of our first newly shared activities. Before long, we discovered that there was a higher connection between food and cooking and our well-being than either of us had realized. By necessity, cooking became a form of therapy by which we began to heal our relationship.

In sacred texts from all over the world, we learned about the secret energies of food and the hidden meaning behind the act of cooking itself. We discovered that cooking can be a joy, an oasis, a peaceful haven from the worries and burdens of daily life.

When Robin returned to the tranquillity of her home kitchen, she developed a new, healthier relationship with food. She also turned to writing, so she could share what she had learned about food with others. She is now a respected expert in vegetarian cooking, with a food column and five cookbooks to her credit.

We concluded that it was time to address the mental and emotional side of what it is we are doing when we enter a kitchen to cook dinner. With Robin's many years of experience cooking the classic cuisines, and Jon's background as an author, editor, and researcher in the ancient wisdom traditions, we are pleased to offer this new approach to enhancing the way people will cook, eat, and live their lives in the twenty-first century.

Many of the ideas presented in this book may seem new, because it aims to take healthy food out of the realm of fads and stereotypes and prepare it beautifully using the techniques of classic Eastern and Western cooking. In reality, the concepts presented in *The Sacred Kitchen* are ancient, because the nutritional and spiritual principles on which the book is based are older than can be measured. They were once second nature to us. Now, they must be relearned, so we can restore sanity to our hectic world.

Living in this new millennium will require a flexible attitude to adapt to an ever-shifting code of ethics, a deluge of information and often contrary advice, a continuing change in our scientific and social paradigms, and a need for genuine intimacy. We need a new strategy, one that will not consume even more precious hours in an already hectic day, but that can set us free by salvaging the time we spend cooking and dining, and making it special and protected.

To accomplish this, our book draws from scriptural sources, religious philosophy, and every tradition in which a spark of wisdom encourages us to live healthier, more fulfilling lives. We show you how to apply the tools we have found in these traditions and synthesize them into practical steps for improving your life and the lives of those you love. The concepts are accessible to anyone who cooks — without requiring the reader to study systems of thought or memorize a foreign language.

This book shows you how to achieve centeredness to free yourself from stress, to be mindful of the moment to alleviate worry, and to stay focused and peaceful while you cook. It helps you "get into the act" of cooking and look forward to dinnertime, not as another chore in your busy day, but as a haven for relaxation and recharging.

The Sacred Kitchen is a new kind of spiritual and culinary adventure in which delicious ingredients are used to create innovative healing recipes. Along the way, we will look at various dietary traditions as well as new medical discoveries and come up with an approach to diet that we call centered cuisine. The recipes are designed to spur your imagination to grow beyond your own expectations and apply new understanding to your everyday cooking — and living.

Included in these pages are over fifty international vegetarian recipes, ranging from meatless versions of classic and favorite dishes to some unique innovative creations that Robin has developed to exemplify the principles in this book. She also provides useful information about ingredients and cooking processes for centered cuisine. You will find inspiring anecdotes, mealtime prayers, quotations by experts, and many exciting secrets for conscientiously cooking with love and energy. We also present a new feast day — The Feast of Light — which is a celebration of the universal reverence for light that anyone can use, regardless of his or her religious beliefs. We believe that when you transform cooking from mechanical drudgery into a celebration of life, you can have a tangible healing effect on your health and the well-being of those who eat your cooking.

The Sacred Kitchen is designed to lift you to a higher consciousness of the energy of food, the miracle of cooking, your connection to the planetary mother, and your co-relationship with the Divine when you cook. These chapters explore cooking as a sacred alchemy that can enhance your life, provide an atmosphere conducive to healing, and bring your family, friends, and partners closer.

So let's claim what we already possess: our inner space. Our own minds and hearts. Let's also reclaim elements of our lives that have become so utilitarian as to be forgotten and taken for granted. The kitchen is one of those elements. We have to cook and use the kitchen, so why not turn kitchen tasks into healing opportunities and discover the sacredness of cooking with a higher consciousness?

We hope this book helps you open your eyes and see your kitchen in a new light. Make it your very own sacred kitchen, a holy temple that can take on a powerful new role in your household. We hope you discover, as a result, that cooking is no longer a chore or source of stress, but a divine ritual and beautiful healing force, not only in your home, but in your community and for the entire planet.

Our prayer for the world is that all families may be free of disease caused by diet, be more centered in their hearts and minds, and be in closer communication with the Creator. May every kitchen become a sacred kitchen, and every dish burst with life force amplified to new heights by enlightened cooks.

1

Heart, Head, and Hands

To see a world in a grain of sand
And heaven in a wild flower
Hold infinity in the palm of your hand
And eternity in an hour.

— William Blake, *Auguries of Innocence*

Kitchens have always served a sacred function. After all, the Creator's promise to all the living — life itself — is sustained there. By honoring the sacredness of the kitchen in an intentional way, we cannot only create a sacred space in which to heal ourselves from the day's concerns, but we can enhance our spiritual lives as well.

Creating a sacred kitchen is an adventure of discovery that begins with our food and our hands, because of the subtle forces that are at work every time we cook. Understanding those forces and learning to feel them are the first steps in creating a sacred kitchen for higher-consciousness cooking. This chapter focuses on how to find peace in the life force of food and tap into it to create a positive experience from start to finish.

"WHERE'S DINNER?"

At the end of a busy day, this nagging question is sometimes the last straw. You give your all by midday, whether working downtown or at home. You try to adapt to the pressure and race the clock all day to keep up. You squeeze in a movie here, a game of tennis there, but the nervous system never really disconnects from the planning, anticipation, competition, worry, and fear of day-to-day living and trying to manage your time. Where did all these concerns come from and how did they build up like this? Your parents (or at least your grandparents) didn't have to live the way we do in the harried 1990s, with our competitive, stress-filled lives.

Over time, you may lose your grip on what should be natural, healthy, and relaxing in your life. You may grow out of touch with your relationships, with your own ideals and dreams, with family members, and even with your job. You've been told that stress can kill you. The warning signs are everywhere that you need to free yourself from it, so you look for ways to give yourself a break.

You can cut only so many corners at work and still get the job done. You wouldn't short-change your loved ones, sending them off to work or school half-dressed and hungry. But at dinnertime, maybe you don't mind cheating a little. After all, you have enablers: the microwave, convenience foods, take-out. Getting it done and cleaned up is now your desperate last chore before you finally earn yourself a rest. It's your chance to really save some time, take a shortcut, and still get something on the table. Amen.

If you have ever felt this way, you know in your heart that your body and mind can't take this pace forever. It's neither healthy for you nor for those who depend on you. At the same time, there's nothing more important than your health. Medical science has shown that a good diet and freedom from stress are vital to well-being and longevity. This is because our mental and physical health — our very ability to survive the hectic pace — are directly related to how and what we eat.

In *Recovering the Soul*, Larry Dossey, M.D., writes: "Today it is

From morning till night, sounds drift from the kitchen, most of them familiar and comforting . . . On days when warmth is the most important need of the human heart, the kitchen is the place you can find it; it dries the wet sock, it cools the hot little brain.

— E.B. White

estimated that the leading causes of death in our society — heart disease, high blood pressure, cancer, and accidents — are directly related to the way we live. Diseases of lifestyle are predicted to continue to be the biggest menace to life as we enter the next century."

If only our need to relax, nourish our bodies, and recharge our spirits could be brought into harmony and work together without becoming just another task during a busy day. By applying the principles in *The Sacred Kitchen*, we can regain what we have lost by discovering a new world in the kitchen and by uncovering hidden secrets about food and the way we prepare it. We can realize how to use our kitchen work to conquer stress, change our attitudes, reverse our dread of chores, and discover the healing that is available to us — right there in our own home. As long as we have to make dinner anyway, let it be a celebration of life, a haven of quality time, and a sacred act that celebrates the connection between cooking and our spiritual health.

Just for the moment, instead of asking "Where's dinner?" let's ask "*What's* dinner?" There's more to it than mere biochemistry: getting the nutritional units into the hungry body. There is a vibrant, subtle energy in everything alive — from a head of lettuce to a person. Let's find out what this energy is and how we use it every day. Sacredness in the kitchen, after all, begins with this very energy — and it's been there all along.

THE LIFE FORCE

Food is life for earthly beings: human, animal, and plant. The fact is, animals and plants would survive just fine without us — but we wouldn't survive for long without them. Plants draw their nourishment from the ground, and animals and humans alike draw nourishment from those plants, ideally when they are still vibrantly alive and fresh with energy. Looking at the hidden truths about food and the secrets of its mystical properties can help us turn our cooking lives around — and the rest of our lives as well.

It is well known among scientists and vegetable gardeners that fresh vegetables and grains possess the purest nutritional value. But they also possess something else that is not readily acknowl-

> That's what the sacred is all about. It's not a concept but an experience — an experience of awe, of wonder, of beauty. And with the sacred comes the zeal, the energy.
>
> — Matthew Fox,
> *Recapture the Sacred*

edged in the West: There is a vibrant hidden energy in every living thing, known as the "life force."

Exactly what is the "life force"? Is it a tribal superstition or a legend? Is it merely the "heat" released by the chemical reactions in a cell? No, say the traditions of Asian medicine, Western scientists, and a growing number of medical doctors such as Deepak Chopra, Andrew Weil, and C. Norman Shealy, founder of the American Holistic Medical Association. This force is the *élan vital* that permeates all of life. Physics continues to refine its concept of a multidimensional universe with terms such as nonlocal, morphogenic, or the "superluminal connectedness" of all things that exists within and beyond our immediate perception. How shocked the scientific world will be when, one day, their theories unite with what the mystical traditions have known for thousands of years.

Amazingly, most traditions acknowledge that energy is everywhere. The Hindus call it by its Sanskrit name, *prana*. In Jewish theology it's called *ruach*, or *vital energy*. In Latin, it is *spiritus* and in Greek, *pneuma*. In Japan, the life force is called *ki*. In China, this same energy is called *chi* (pronounced *chee*). Chi is the word for "breath," and the Chinese ideogram for chi can be thought of as depicting a pot of cooking rice — the life force as contained in food. (see Figure 1.1).

Chi: Energy or Life Force

The ideogram shows the asterisk-like fire generating and releasing the steam/energy above. It can be thought of as a metaphor for a pot of cooking rice.

Figure 1.1

Chi permeates everything in our world: the soil, water, fire, and air. First seen scientifically in Kirlian photography, this energy is present in "auras." According to Taoist teacher Mantak Chia, "Chi is the glue between our body, mind, and spirit, the link between our perception of the inner and outer worlds."

Natural, unprocessed vegetables, fruits, and grains are especially rich in chi. Certainly, these foods contain the nutritional fuel

Taoist Cultivation of Chi

Chi pre-existed before everything in the physical world as original chi, or pure energy. This neatly avoided disagreements about the metaphysical nature of original chi and focused attention on its functional manifestation in the ordinary world, as hot yang chi in fresh garlic or weak yin chi in a diseased liver. As a result, Taoist philosophy tends to be very pragmatic and grounded in observation of the natural organic world. Taoist cultivation of chi energy may extend into what may at first glance appear to be impossibly subtle spiritual realms, but it always begins with down-to-earth and in-the-body practices.

— Mantak Chia and Michael Winn, *Taoist Secrets of Love*

that our bodies burn. But we also receive the chi they contain when we eat them, which then flows throughout our bodies, organs, and the networks of energy pathways called meridians by acupuncturists. Chi circulates in the body, and the amount and quality of our chi affects the aura. Chi strengthens and wanes, depending on the quality of the food we eat and our body's health, or its ability to absorb chi from the food.

The body's cells spend their food, burning it as energy. The body also spends the life force with the mind, as we project our thoughts and emotions. When we replenish our nutrients, we must also recharge our body and mind with the life force: the living, loving divine energy that vibrates among the atoms and

God's message does not come only in words. What comes in words is small compared with the radiance the message brings to all things and all beings. It comes in the form of a sacrament, as bread and wine, and bread and wine symbolize life and love.

— Hazrat Inayat Khan
The Sufi Message,

molecules. When we allow this energy level to dwindle, for example, through stress, we can feel out of touch, unhealthy, lacking in vitality, mentally sluggish, and emotionally depressed.

Food quality plays an important role in our life force. The more "alive" the food we eat, the more rich it is in chi. Freezing, refrigeration, and chemical preservatives extend the shelf life of food, and proponents of irradiation claim the process can preserve food indefinitely. But just as aging food loses its vitamin potency, it also loses its life force. Processing further diminishes its value. The fresher the food, the closer we come to the pure healing energy of the earth's own chi and the higher the benefit to our bodies and minds. This is the first key to discovering the connection

Seeing the Life Force

Seeing is believing. Let your imaginative forces work freely as you recline under a clear, blue sky. At first, close your eyes and take several deep refreshing breaths. When you open your eyes to the sky, you may see some retinal marking or blood cell shadows, but beyond them is chi, prana, the life force, gliding as particles, floating and pulsing like tiny bubbles. Breathe deeply, and try not to judge or disbelieve. Just be the observer. The chi is all around. Knowing this, let the evidence of its presence merrily effervesce over the entire background field.

Now slowly turn your attention to trees or shrubbery that may be leaning overhead into your view. Look at the edges first, and note the difference there. The difference is the life force emanating from the trees. Some people will only distinguish a change from the background, while others will see a light aura of differing colors. Still others will see surprisingly dramatic energy patterns radiating from the trees. Take another deep breath. Sit upright. Examine leaves and plants up close, either held against the sky or light background, and allow yourself to see the energy in living plants. With practice, the life force will reveal itself to you: in animals and people, grass and birds, and in the vegetables you are preparing for your meal.

between higher-consciousness cooking and our spiritual health: All food contains this powerful life force.

Why don't we normally see the chi in the world around us? Why don't most of us see auras? The answer has to do with our training and the way we perceive the world. Especially in the West, people focus on the outside world of objects and phenomena or the intellectual world of ideas, and place little importance on feelings or intuitive information. It just takes awareness and a little practice to tune in to the inner antennae that we haven't been using. An excellent exercise for this purpose is the Seeing the Life Force exercise on page 6.

Ideally, every meal should contain foods that are alive with energy-fresh grains and vegetables. For this reason, organically grown food is best, for it has had little processing and is ostensibly chemical-free. In reality, the best meal we can eat is made from living ingredients skillfully combined, the life force conveyed deliciously for use in our bodies. We will look more closely at the value of fresh foods in chapter 4, but there is something more to explore about chi and its role in the sacred kitchen.

HANDS AND HEARTS

The ingredients being prepared for a meal possess their own life force, but another hidden energy that most people overlook is also present in every meal: that energy comes from *you*. You possess your own chi, and the food absorbs energy directly from you when you cook.

Studies of the human energy field have been ongoing for thousands of years. The first record of it was by Pythagoras around 500 B.C., who noted that it could be manipulated to cure illness. Various philosophers during the Middle Ages explored evidence of universal forces. In the later centuries of the second millennium A.D., scientists explored electromagnetic forces and how bodies can influence other bodies through the invisible fluid exchanges of vital forces. In the twentieth century, various scientists and medical doctors have also explored the universal energy field.

In *Hands of Light*, NASA scientist turned psychotherapist/heal-

Each morning I think of the farmers out in the fields of Pennsylvania and I think of the Indians of Chiapas growing the coffee for my morning cup. I feel connected to them through an economic system based on respect and care. We are connected both spiritually and economically.

— Judy Wicks, multicultural activist and owner of The White Dog Café, Philadelphia, Pennsylvania

Love is the face and body of the universe. It is the connective tissue of the universe, the stuff of which we are made. Love is the experience of being whole and connected to universal divinity.

— Barbara Ann Brennan, *Hands of Light*

er Barbara Ann Brennan writes, "The Human Energy Field is the manifestation of universal energy that is intimately involved with human life. It can be described as a luminous body that surrounds and interpenetrates the physical body, emits its own characteristic radiation and is usually called the 'aura.'" She describes how she discovered this as a child playing in the woods, but that only after her training as a scientist and psychotherapist later in life did she learn "to interact with it consciously, as with anything else I can see. I could manipulate my own field to interact with another person's field."

Universal energy — chi — is naturally pure, clean, and centered. Neither earth, air, water, nor garden are ever angry or resentful. People, however, tend to color, shape, and pollute their life energy through their attitudes, emotions, and thoughts. When you introduce your own chi to the mixing bowl, you unknowingly convey subtle, imperceptible influences into the food as a result of your attitude.

The fact is, when your hands physically join with the ingredients as you prepare them, you convey the vibration, the energy of your life force directly into the food. Moreover, your energy is colored by what you are thinking and feeling as you cook. Whenever you cook, you should always keep in mind the amazing alchemy taking place between the energies of the ingredients and the energies of your heart, head, and hands. These are important keys in understanding the connection between your kitchen and your spiritual life. In our modern world, we must all rediscover them even though they have been with us since the first humans scratched their bellies and looked around for something to eat.

Grasses, grains, fruits, and vegetables first grew in the wild wherever the wind and the birds scattered their seeds. But some prehistoric gardener figured out that when planted, food could be cultivated and harvested. Ever since that day, the life force in food has been shaped by human consciousness. This human effect upon food begins at the grassroots level — down on the farm or in your backyard garden. But in the hands of a cook, the energies can have a subtle though specific impact on health and mood.

What that first gardener discovered was a matter of observation. However, when the first person pounded the seeds she'd collected in the meadow, added water, and baked the result, she created the miracle of bread. Even if the kids had been a handful that day, she was running on pure inspiration. She'd been awakened to the spirit of the life force in the grain and transformed it, as bread, into a new entity, its life force amplified.

As long as society stayed simple, people cooked food simply. Along the way, new innovations of leavenings, spices, and ingredients emerged, but getting dinner on the table didn't change much for many millennia. A prehistoric mother, feeling edgy because her village had just been sacked, may have hidden some wholesome, living ingredients to feed her family later. Food quality wasn't a problem. Today, our frantic lifestyle requires more than just stirring the stew over a wood fire. We want the taste of home cooking, but we also want the convenience of take-out. Whether you dine out or order in, dinner is often artificial, processed, and microwaveable.

We'd like to see a formal study initiated to determine the effects of meals cooked under different conditions. In such an experiment, two cooks would prepare the same meal. One cook, in a peaceful, templelike space, would concentrate on feeling love for the diners, with soothing, harmonious music playing. The other cook would gather rancor and hate for the recipients, while listening to nerve-rattling discordant music in a squalid kitchen. With the proper controls, perhaps a correlation between the cooks' attitudes and the diners' moods and energy levels could be documented.

Even if such effects can't be measured in a scientific experiment, it doesn't take a scientist to compare the peaceful hearts who quietly reside in ashrams and retreats with the frustrated road-rage society struggling through life elsewhere. The fact is, food prepared lovingly and joyfully by someone who enjoys cooking will taste better to those eating it, while charging them with an enhanced, healing life force.

We have personally observed this effect in our own informal experiments on unsuspecting dinner guests in our home. We have seen people "awaken" as they eat a meal that Robin has prepared with a healing purpose.

Essence, chi, and spirit are the three jewels of life.

— Master Ni Hua Ching,
The Book of Changes and the Unchanging Truth

During the summer of 1991, we met a woman who had been recently diagnosed with a particularly debilitating form of cancer. The disease had only just begun to manifest a few months before, so she was still ambulatory, yet frequently afflicted with exhaustion and waves of discomfort over her body. She had lost her appetite and was losing weight. Pam and her partner had agreed to come to our house for dinner, and Robin set out to test the idea of infusing the food with as much love and healing power as possible.

Robin made a simple dinner of stir-fried brown rice with fresh vegetables, miso soup, and a couscous cake for dessert. With a menu chosen for maximum healing and nutrition, she prayed before she began to cook and opened her mind and heart to direct healing energy through her hands until the meal was ready.

Pam barely ate at home, and her partner was worried about her. But once she began to eat this meal, she was overwhelmed by an increasing hunger, and she did not stop eating until she had devoured three platefuls. Pam later reported that she felt better overall for several days afterward, and we were convinced of the power of the life force when used with purpose and intention.

Other friends who normally only pick at their food have told Robin that there was "something" about the meal she had served that they just couldn't pinpoint — but that helped them feel better well into the following day.

Is it any wonder that we still yearn for "Mom's home cooking" and not the food that was dished out to us in high school, the local lunch counter, or fast-food restaurant? How much did Mom love us as we were heading off to school or work? How much of that love energy passed through her hands and into our breakfasts, lunches, and dinners?

Cooking can be a way of "giving of yourself." How better to express love, either through the act that creates life, or through the act that sustains life? This is what cooking ought to be. As you strive to balance your body through a more healthful diet, how much better will your life be if you also strive for this fresh new attitude? Realizing the importance of attitude can help transform us all into creative practitioners — artists and healers — when we go into the kitchen to cook. A change of attitude can benefit every other aspect of our lives.

THE ALCHEMY OF ATTITUDE

The type of energy we convey to the food when we cook depends entirely on our attitude. This classic story from Southern India illustrates how, when we keep our attitude pure, our cooking experience actually approaches the Divine.

There once lived a husband and wife who had prayed to God all their married lives to have a son. Lord Shiva finally granted them their son, but only on the condition that he would never live past his twenty-fifth birthday.

Their son grew to become a handsome, healthy, intelligent young man. When it became time for him to marry, his father went to great lengths to find a suitable bride. Finally, he found the daughter of a devoutly religious family and, feeling satisfied, made the arrangements for the wedding. At first, the young man's mother lamented that it might be cruel to marry him to a woman who would be widowed so soon, but his father insisted that everything would work out fine.

The couple was married and the years passed. As the young man approached his twenty-fifth birthday, however, his mother became filled with sadness. But the father remained strangely calm, assuring his wife that nothing would happen. The dreaded day came and went without incident. Day after day passed, and the young man's mother was relieved, but puzzled. How could it be? Lord Shiva himself had fixed the date. The father, seeing that his wife was concerned, suggested that she come along with him to their son's house, and maybe they would find the answer.

They arrived before dawn and stood outside a window where, in the dim light of the small kitchen, they could see their young daughter-in-law preparing breakfast for her husband. They watched as she churned the butter, and with every rotation of the churn, she chanted, "Shiva." Then she placed the butter in a pan on the stove, and as she stirred the melting butter, she sang, "Shiva, Shiva." Likewise, as she chopped the onions, the name of the god was on her lips. As she folded the spices into the soft dough of her bread, her clear, sweet voice chanted lovingly, "Shiva, Shiva, Shiva."

The meal, over which she had labored for several hours, was served, and her husband ate it enthusiastically before going off to work. As his parents returned home, the woman said to the man, "It was nice to see our daughter-in-law serving her husband with such devotion, but I don't understand how it is that he is still alive."

He explained, "My dear, it is true that Lord Shiva decreed that our son's life was to be limited, but even Lord Shiva must heed the prayers of his devotees. You saw the way that woman prayed to Lord Shiva as she fixed the food. Her prayers went right into the food itself. Each day, death is waiting to grab our son, and each day he eats that food and death has to stay away. As long as they keep up this divine routine, our son cannot die."

What the elderly couple in this story discovered reveals the heart and soul of how we can free ourselves to transform our

The Food of Love

We are permeated by the food of light, vibrations, air, and water. We are nourished by the food of plants. We are sustained by the food of love, by the endless love of our Heavenly Father and Earthly Mother. We are inspired by the interpretation of that love through music, art, and the beauty of nature.

When we take this food into ourselves, let us first consider whether or not we are worthy of it. Let us then receive it in gratitude and offer it back to the spirit from whence it came. In receiving and returning this offering of food, let us be certain that it is worthy of us, that it is pure and carrying the life force it is meant to carry. Let us consider whether the food we eat is worthy of the Great Spirit of the universe and of the same Great Spirit, or God, which we carry within.

— Cecile Tovah Levin, *Cooking for Regeneration*

cooking lives into a sacred adventure. It's the idea, known for millennia in the East, that our happiness and health are dependent on our attitude. If we attempt to transcend our materialistic confusion and artificial complaints, we can actually change the world through the way we cook and eat.

Ron Pickarski is a chef, author, and former Franciscan monk who calls himself a food missionary. In his book, *Eco-Cuisine*, he writes, "In the preparation and eating of food, human and divine action is required. Matter and spirit are united in the food by which they subsist. When I am in the kitchen, either to create new recipes or cook a dinner, my work becomes a spiritual discipline. Culinary art is my spiritual path, the way I commune with God and humanity through the forces of nature."

The pen is mightier than the sword, but the spoon is the most powerful of the three.

Whether you live in Southern India, North Africa, or East Lansing, you can change your life just by taking a look at what really goes on inside your sauté pan — as well as what goes on inside you — when you cook. Imagine. Just by preparing yourself to give total, joyful attention to your cooking, you can heal yourself and those around you.

This point is amplified in Laura Esquivel's novel *Like Water for Chocolate*, which tells the story of Tita, the young daughter of a Mexican family who is in love with a young man forbidden to her. By arrangement, Pedro is betrothed to her older sister, Rosaura. The quiet Tita does most of the cooking for the large household, and the guests invariably fall under the influence of what Tita is feeling when she cooks.

Forced to prepare the wedding cake for Rosaura and Pedro's wedding, heartsick Tita cries as she cooks, her tears dripping sadly into the cake batter. When wedding guests take their first bite of the tear-filled cake, they are overcome with deep sadness and inexplicable longing. They are moved to tears, suddenly crying over their own lost loves. The wedding guests could not understand how sadness had descended on them on such a happy occasion.

Later in the story, Pedro gives Tita a bouquet of roses — an act that brings disapproval from Tita's mother and sister. So tightly

> If there is no meal there is no Torah, if there is no Torah there is no meal.
>
> — The Talmud,
> *Sayings of the Fathers*

does Tita clench the forbidden roses to her chest that the thorns scratch her hands and breasts, and the roses turn from pink to red with the blood from her cut flesh. But rather than throw away the roses given by her true love, Tita decides to use the petals to make a sauce for dinner that night. The combination of Pedro's loving rose petals and Tita's blood causes a mystical interaction of their desire for each other. When the family later begins to eat the sumptuous meal of quail in rose petal sauce, Tita and Pedro find they are able to silently communicate their passion for each other while eating this meal. Their unrequited desire, however, is also absorbed by Tita's other sister, Gertrudis, who is inexplicably overwhelmed as though by a powerful aphrodisiac.

Esquivel's story is told in the magical realism idiom of Mexican and South American literature, and it depicts a subtle reality that operates unnoticed within us all: Our attitude projects itself out into the world and into the lives of others, whether we want it to or not. Thoughts are things, as the saying goes. Through our attitude, we can give to those we love a little bit of the energy of that love, transmitted from our hearts through our hands as we cook. We can enhance the benefit of this effect by purposefully focusing it.

However you pray, ask God to direct loving energy through you when you cook to charge the food with a higher energy to heal everyone you are feeding. Above all, prepare yourself before cooking by entering the kitchen only after you have released tensions and negative feelings. Do this with an excited anticipation for the time you will spend there and the miracle that you are about to create.

There are a number of ways in which you can infuse the food with love and healing energy:

- Ritually wash and bless your hands.
- Calm your mind with three deep breaths.
- Utter a simple personal prayer to align yourself with spirit.
- Ask for peace of mind and heart.
- Say aloud: "Lord, I affirm my holiness as I prepare this meal."
- Use soothing music as a focus.

- Visualize healing white energy flowing from your head through your hands.
- Maintain a prayerful attitude throughout the cooking process.

The underlying secret to having a sacred kitchen is to realize that cooking should be more than just getting food on the table. When its power and possibilities are fully understood, cooking is *food alchemy*. Begin to have respect for the hidden power of cooking, and realize that it's not just "another chore" but a sacred act patterned after Creation itself. Think of cooking as a sacred science as well as a sacred art.

SEEING YOUR KITCHEN WITH NEW EYES

The key to creating a sacred kitchen in your house is changing your attitude toward it. Realize the divine nature of the forces involved: the life force in food, the contribution of your own energies, and your ability to convey divine energy into the meal.

To physically make the sacred kitchen a part of your home, you need to make its higher, subtle meaning a new part of your consciousness. Begin creating new habits now by consciously thinking about your kitchen as a sacred place. Old habits are hard to break, especially ones that push your buttons or alter your feelings over and over. If you cannot change a workday that brings you home in a foul mood, then changing your attitude toward it is the only solution. Let the sacred kitchen help by becoming something to look forward to during the day and on waking up in the morning.

In the next three chapters, we look at ways to make changes in the physical space of the kitchen, in how we think and behave in the kitchen, and in our diet. The sooner you realize your kitchen's new sacred role, the better. For now, post an image of something that has sacred meaning to you on the kitchen door or at the doorway. This can be an angel, or some other symbol of your belief system (a crucifix, mezuzah, prayer wheel, etc.) — anything placed there to remind you that you are entering a holy space.

Consciously work toward establishing new habits while in your kitchen. Remember that we only change our habits when it becomes important enough. For example, we may change our diet when the doctor tells us to or when what we see in the mirror so disgusts us that we decide to lose some weight. It's time now to envision the kitchen as the sacred place it was meant to be, because of the miracles of alchemy you will perform there and the divine life force the food contains.

Think of your newly discovered sacred kitchen as a:

- Conscious choice
- Personal commitment
- New awareness
- Joyful practice
- Haven of peace

Begin now to eagerly anticipate the next time you are going to cook, and the wonderful new changes you can make in your life as you apply the principles of *The Sacred Kitchen*. Try to keep the above points in mind by posting them on your dresser or on your desk at work, to remind yourself that your kitchen is your new restful daily haven: a place where you are going to learn to relax, and to heal yourself and those who depend on you.

In our society, we need to rediscover that simpler lifestyle when mealtime was a vital focus of the day, not a stressful interruption. Even with today's hectic schedules, with our health and well-being at stake, mealtime can be considered a priority: a joy instead of a burden. This is the kitchen fulfilling its true role as a sacred temple.

Whether you live alone or with a partner, you can prepare and eat your meal with a more conscious intent by purchasing the freshest food available and honoring the preparation time you spend with these gifts of the earth — just as they were grown, rich with nutrition and an energy all their own. Let this time be spent gratefully in the presence of those ingredients and, like a master alchemist, infuse them with love. Then, sit by and watch as all those who eat your food grow, heal, and thrive around you. It's all right to take quiet pleasure in that.

Changing the way you cook and eat requires timing, planning, and patience. When you've been used to cooking a certain way for many years, and then you suddenly decide to create a major shift, it makes sense to expect resistance until you establish a new routine. But if your old routine only added to your stress, then let these new ideas be a welcome change in your life. And be patient with yourself — the change will be gradual.

Achieving a positive attitude is a matter of bringing peace into your heart before you enter the kitchen. Let kitchen work no longer be a chore, but a blessing that brings you peace and healing. Look for and find joy in every aspect of cooking, not just is serving and eating — yes, even in the washing of the lettuce and the cleaning up afterward.

This is well illustrated in a ritual practiced in Zen monasteries called "rice-washing contemplation." It is an exercise in which, as the monk washes the rice, he purges from his mind all thoughts unrelated to meal preparation. In this way, the monk can focus his energies on the food he is about to prepare. Soei Yoneda, abbess of Tokyo's Sanko-in Temple and author of *The Heart of Zen Cuisine*, states, "I am convinced that this spiritual attitude toward cooking — being totally present to what you are doing and allowing no distractions — is valid anywhere in the world and that its application will bring any cooking to perfection." Rice-washing contemplation is a good mental discipline that can also help you relax and raise your consciousness to the subtle beauty in the rice and flowing water. This practice can be extended to other kitchen chores as well.

Begin today. Whenever you wash rice, knead dough, or cut vegetables, focus your thoughts only on the task at hand. This will help you clear your mind and release the tensions of the day. Think of this time apart as a kind of meditation. Be "mindful" and "in the moment," techniques that are explored further in chapter 4. Allow the task to energize and relax you, and you can continue this relaxed attitude throughout the meal and beyond.

With this new attitude toward kitchen work, we can take a

Not surprisingly, incivility, insensitivity, and ingratitude learned at the family table can infect all other aspects of one's life. Conversely, good habits and thoughtful attitudes regarding food and eating will have far-reaching benefits.

— Leon R. Kass, M.D,
The Hungry Soul

close look at the next important aspect of higher-consciousness cooking: the physical space of your kitchen and your attitude when you cook.

RECIPES TO FEEL THE LIFE FORCE

As you make the following recipes, think about the principles of this chapter, especially the benefits of putting them into practice. The First-Sign-of-Spring Rolls, made with fresh-picked ingredients, if possible, are a great way to honor the chi described in the Seeing the Life Force exercise on page 6. They are especially good with the accompanying Peanut Sauce. Favoring Curry is the entrée, a sublime vegetable curry that provides another showcase for fresh vegetables. Serve the curry over Brown Rice with Love and, when you prepare the rice, use the rice-washing contemplation described on page 17. To add a finishing touch to this meal, try the refreshing Grilled Pineapple with Mango Coulis for dessert.

FIRST-SIGN-OF-SPRING ROLLS

Spring rolls are so called because they are an important part of Chinese New Year feasts held each spring. Because they are made with raw vegetables, these spring rolls are high in chi. Prepare this recipe after practicing the Seeing the Life Force exercise to learn awareness of the chi energy. These spring rolls are especially delicious when served with peanut sauce. Rice wrappers are similar to eggroll wrappers but need no cooking. They are available at Asian markets and are usually round rather than square.

Twelve 6-inch rice wrappers
12 small leaf lettuce leaves
12 snow peas, trimmed and cut into thin strips
1 cup fresh bean sprouts
1 cup grated carrot
2 scallions, chopped

The light that shines beyond the heavens and above this world, the light that shines in the highest world, beyond which there are no others, is the same light that shines in the hearts of men.

— The Chandogya-Upanishad, III.13.7f.

24 enoki mushrooms, trimmed
1 tablespoon minced fresh cilantro, plus 12 fresh
    cilantro sprigs (for garnish)
Peanut Sauce (recipe follows)

Immerse the rice wrappers one at a time in a bowl filled with cold water and let stand until the wrapper softens and turn white. Spread a kitchen towel on a work surface and place each wrapper on top of the towel.

To assemble the rolls, place lettuce leaf on each wrapper, allowing the lettuce to extend beyond the top of the wrapper. Arrange strips of snow peas, bean sprouts, carrot, scallion, mushrooms, and minced cilantro on the wrapper about midway between the edge nearest you and the center of the wrapper. Fold the edge nearest you over the vegetables, then fold in one side and roll up lengthwise into a tight roll. Repeat with the remaining wrappers.

To serve, arrange 2 rolls on each plate, garnish with 2 cilantro sprigs, and serve with a small bowl of peanut sauce.

Serves 6

Peanut Sauce

Serve this creamy dipping sauce in small bowls alongside the First-Sign-of-Spring Rolls. The chili paste can be adjusted to suit your preferred level of hotness.

4 tablespoons creamy peanut butter
2 tablespoons tamari sauce
2 tablespoons water
1 teaspoon sugar, or a natural sweetener
$^1/_2$ teaspoon chile paste

In a small bowl or blender, stir or blend all the ingredients together until well combined. Taste and adjust the seasoning. Use now, or cover and refrigerate for up to 2 weeks.

Makes $1/2$ cup

FAVORING CURRY

The types of vegetables used may be altered to suit availability and personal taste. Cooked chickpeas or cubed firm tofu may be added to this dish for extra protein, if desired.

    1 tablespoon canola oil
    1 $1/2$ tablespoons curry powder or paste
    $1/2$ teaspoon ground cumin
    $1/2$ teaspoon ground cinnamon
    $1/8$ teaspoon cayenne pepper
    $3/4$ cup water
    2 garlic cloves, minced
    1 small onion, chopped
    1 large carrot, chopped
    1 yellow bell pepper, seeded, deribbed, and chopped
    2 cups fresh or frozen green peas
    $1/3$ cup coconut milk
    Salt to taste
    1 tablespoon minced fresh cilantro or parsley
    Brown Rice with Love (recipe follows)

Heat the oil in a large skillet over medium-high heat. Add the curry powder or paste, cumin, cinnamon, and cayenne and stir until fragrant, about 30 seconds. Add the water, garlic, onion, carrot, and bell pepper. Reduce heat to low. Cover and cook, stirring occasionally, for 10 minutes, or until the vegetables have softened. Add the peas, coconut milk, and salt and simmer, uncovered, for

One should eat to live, not live to eat.

— Molière, *The Miser*

5 minutes. Remove from heat and transfer to a serving bowl. Sprinkle with cilantro or parsley and serve over brown rice.

Serves 4

Brown Rice with Love

Before you make the following recipe, prepare yourself by feeling love for all those who are going to eat the meal. Try to feel the life force filling your hands with pure energy as you measure out and wash the grain and combine the ingredients. Allow the love for those you will feed to travel down your arms and into the rice, and don't allow any negative thoughts to distract you. Short-grain brown rice is used because of its delightful chewy texture and nutty flavor. Long-grain brown rice may be substituted, which only needs to cook for 30 minutes.

    3 cups short-grain brown rice
    8 cups water
    1 teaspoon sea salt

Rinse and drain the rice. Bring the water to a boil in a covered pot. Add the salt. Add the rice, cover, and reduce heat to medium-low. Simmer for 45 minutes, or until tender. Drain in a sieve. Run cold water through the cooked rice for a few seconds.

Makes 6 cups

GRILLED PINEAPPLE WITH MANGO COULIS

Choose the ripest fruit available for maximum flavor and natural sweetness. Rely on your sense of smell to pick a fresh pineapple — its sweet aroma will tell you if it is ripe. Ripe mangos yield slightly to the touch when gently pressed.

$1/_4$ cup sugar, or a natural sweetener
1 cup cubed mango
$1/_4$ cup mango juice
1 teaspoon fresh lemon juice
1 pineapple, peeled, cored and cut into $1/_2$-inch slices
1 cup strawberries, hulled and sliced

In a blender or food processor, combine the sugar or other sweetener, mango, mango juice and lemon juice, and blend well. Transfer to a small serving bowl and set aside. Preheat the broiler and grill the pineapple slices on both sides. Arrange the pineapple slices on a pool of mango coulis and scatter the strawberry slices attractively over the fruit and coulis. Pass the remaining coulis separately.

Serves 4

When you eat and take pleasure in the taste and sweetness of the food, bear in mind that it is the Lord who has placed into the food its taste and sweetness. You will, then, truly serve him by your eating.

—The Baal Shem Tov

A Blessing

The food upon my table
Shares its life with me
I ask that this life nourish me,
As I shall one day nourish the earth
With my body
And as I now nourish the earth
With my love.

— Danaan Parry, *The Essene Book of Days*, 1993

2

Kitchen Power

*O Mother Earth, You are the earthly source
of all existence. The fruits which You bear
are the source of life for the Earth peoples.
You are always watching over
Your fruits as does a mother.
May the steps which we take
in life upon You be sacred and not weak.*

— Oglala Sioux prayer

We know that fresh food is rich in the life force and that we can enhance the quality of a meal through our attitude when we cook. Now, we expand our awareness to include the planetary life force and the role it plays in your sacred kitchen. We then look at the dynamics of the kitchen space itself and how you can ensure energy balance in your kitchen through feng shui, the Chinese art of placement. In chapters 3 and 4, we assist you in discovering how to bring balance into your life and your diet. Let's investigate how your kitchen shares in the power of the global kitchen and what you have in common with everyone in the world who is cooking at the same time you are.

THE GLOBAL KITCHEN

When You Enter Your Sacred Kitchen

Think of your role as a maker of miracles, a representative of the Divine Mother, whenever you enter the kitchen space. Wash your hands and say a simple prayer:

Bless, O Lord, the holy work of my kitchen, That I may be worthy to share your gifts with all.

Prepare and clear your mind with three deep breaths, thinking of the life force in the ingredients, the love of your heart that you wish to convey into the meal, and your universal connection with the global kitchen.

If you are one of those people who can lose yourself while making a batch of cookies, wandering among memories of childhood with the first whiff from the oven, then perhaps you are already beginning to see your kitchen as a sacred place. If the kitchen has never meant more to you than the place where you grab your morning coffee or microwave your popcorn, then thinking of your kitchen as a temple may be just what you need to bring more harmony into your life. After all, this is the room in which, no matter what else is going on in the world or how busy your day has been, you are the one in charge. You have the power to take control in the kitchen and make miracles happen there.

Think of how sacred the kitchen is: It's the place where, with some flour, yeast, and water, you can create bread — the staff of life — with your bare hands. Now, take some apples — miracles in their own right. Peel, slice, and place them in a crust, which is like bread, a transformation of flour and water. Sprinkle the slices with sugar and spice, and it becomes a miraculous new entity that transcends the sum of its parts. This new entity possesses an intoxicatingly redolent aroma and a warm, juicy sweetness that dissolves the flaky crumbles on your tongue. Nutrition, yes. Chemistry, sure. But a pie, like any recipe, is a miracle nonetheless. A loaf of bread, a pie, or a pot of ratatouille is like a miraculous healing brought on by prayer, a base metal turned into gold, a loaf divided to feed a multitude.

In your kitchen, you keep yourself and your loved ones alive, and you can contribute directly to the quality of these lives simply by engendering love and a prayerful attitude in your heart when you cook. In the kitchen, your power extends farther, because even when you are cooking by yourself, you are not alone — in that singular act, you are one with the billions of others on earth who are cooking at the same time. You are, in fact, a member of the global kitchen: the worldwide unity of all cooks everywhere. Here's why:

In the uniform sweep of the earth's rotation, the sun continuously creates morning, degree by degree. Visualize the kitchens of the world coming alive in this never-ending wave. Every moment, kitchens, hearths, campfires, and village ovens flicker to life as dawn heralds the beginning of the new day. In this morning twilight, the earth itself is a kitchen: a fertile cook pot of forests and fields, heat, steam, and the rich seasoning of recycled plant and animal life. Like a perpetual pot of *minestra* simmering at the back of a stove in an Italian village, soils, streams, and air continuously stew up Mother Nature's hearty meal that never stops cooking and is always ready to eat.

In the perpetual morning, the world's citizens yawn and shake off their dreams. The beat of hands kneading, knives chopping, and ladles dipping divides each second of the morning into infinity as the rosy horizon brightens. The world is always chewing and swallowing in the perpetual dawn, and power from the mountains of food turns into fuel for the body of humankind that will last until its next meal.

Harvey Diamond, co-creator of the Fit for Life diet, writes in *Your Heart, Your Planet,* "When most of us sit down to eat a meal, we haven't the slightest awareness of how our everyday food choices affect the health of our planet. But, in fact, all things are strongly connected. Everything is part of everything else. Nothing really stands alone. We don't always see the connection between one phenomenon and another, but the planet earth is a living, breathing ecological entity held together by trillions of different occurrences that appear to be separate but are actually highly interconnected."

The planet itself, containing all the food all the time, is the power cell and great heartbeat of the life force. Planetary chi flows over the hills and plains, and among the meadows, grottoes, forests, and mountains. It enlivens the very air in a gentle breeze, a zephyr, or gust. It bursts from the waters, whether they are standing, trickling, rushing, or swelling. The chi in your hands and broccoli is a dip from the well of this planetary chi filling the crucible of your kitchen.

Tomorrow morning, when you shuffle into the kitchen to make breakfast, think about this higher-consciousness power that you share with everyone else cooking in the world. Let this knowledge warm you and inspire you to unveil the reality of the global kitchen in your heart. Think of the bread you are about to toast and the grain it was made from. Those vast, waving miles of life-giving grain are the earth's offspring and they possess a spiritual quality.

"Food is Spirit," writes macrobiotic teacher and author Cecile Tovah Levin in *Cooking for Regeneration*. "It has come to us through the divine intercourse of heaven and earth. The infinite and eternal cosmic vibrations of light-fire have coalesced and crystallized to form the air, water, earth, plants, all creatures and us — they are the very heart and soul of us."

Of all foods, grain most universally exemplifies the connection between you and the global kitchen. Grain is the swelling fruit of the Mother's swaying grasses, collecting the energy of the sun, the Father, and offering its life force as food to all the living. Grain is the seeds of the grasses that cover the world's meadows, prairies, and plains. Waves of green, yellow, and brown take their bows as the wind brushes its soft hands over the earth. Like gold, grain pours into grinding stones from hands black and brown, yellow and white, and red. The sounds of threshing and sifting blend into the great resounding OM in the heart of the universe as flour transforms into cakes and bread. Grain is mother's milk to all, as though the planet had her own kind of intelligence and love for her people. Grain is the staple for most of the world's population. By the measure, grain is brought to the mill, pounding stone, or steaming pot, its glowing life force still shimmering around it like an aura.

Through honest labor, grain is harvested from the field and cascades from winnowing baskets into waiting hands. When next you reach into a bin for a cup of flour, think big. Think of your act as directly connected to the village, community, nation, and planet. In terms of the divinity conveyed in each ingredient in every recipe, that cup of flour represents the earth's inexhaustible pantry.

For an even deeper awareness of the hidden power of grain, try to imagine the canisters and bins in your pantry as miniature versions of the towering granaries of the ancient world. In Egypt, Thebes, and Babylon, grain was used as money to pay debts and taxes. Grain by the heaping bushel was paid as tribute to kings. The granaries of Egypt were committed to Joseph's care after he warned Pharaoh that seven years of plenty would be followed by seven years of drought.

Whenever you prepare grain, let your kitchen be as a temple, your table as an altar. "In the sacred books of the Jewish people," wrote Ben M. Edidin in his classic *Jewish Customs and Ceremonies,* "the table is spoken of as an altar and the act of eating as a sacred rite." Think of it this way: On this table-altar, the life essence of the grain is offered, having been softened, warmed, and transformed by the alchemy of our cooking art, our spices, and love. The life of the grain passes from the earth into our hands, from our pot onto our plate. Its life is now our life, and it shall become life for all those we feed.

Spiritual power is attributed to grain by indigenous peoples the world over. In North America, Native Americans believed that corn was holy. They held corn ceremonies during which they would clean out their houses, atone for past grievances, and extinguish old fires. A new crop commemorated a new beginning for the village. This concept envelops us all as we consume our daily bread and connects us inexorably to the powerful life force of the planet, the "great medicine wheel" that underlies Native American religious belief.

"The Circle of Life, the Great Medicine Wheel," writes Native American writer Jamie Sams in her book *Earth Medicine*, "has no beginning and no end. Every part of creation exists as part of this circle, and each has a purpose. The Native American way of being speaks of a creed that insists on life, unity, equality for eternity. Every person who sits in the Circle has a voice, needed talents, and the right to make the world a better place for all living things. The earthwalk, or life, of each human being will reflect that person's commitment to the whole of creation. Words are empty commitments unless they ring with truth that is backed with positive action."

The power of the kitchen knows no bounds in the household, because life itself is sustained there. Whoever happens to be the cook acts as a nurturer in that household. Whether you are a woman or a man, this role should be taken as a great honor, for you represent a higher nurturer when making dinner.

The Iroquois called beans, squash, and corn the "three sisters." These "crop maidens" were often grown together and eaten together because the beans could climb the corn stalks, and the squash could grow in the mound at their base, producing a shady ground cover. The Zuni and the Hopi sang prayers, held ceremonies, and gave offerings to bless the corn as it grew, believing that the corn was divinely created. To them and other tribes, an ear of corn embodied the spirit of the Corn Mother.

Nourishment from Heaven and Earth

When we take our meals, we must also rest from all external activity, in order to relax and facilitate the internal movement of digestion. The period of separation and distinction between our outer activity and inner activity was ritualized long ago into forms of prayer: the time for offering gratitude for the meal to be received and for receiving grace through the nourishment given from heaven and earth.
In giving thanks for the nourishment that sustains us, we should consider all the forces of heaven and earth, the rain and the

continued

OUR WORKING MOTHER

Higher consciousness of the global kitchen reveals cooking as an alchemical wave that progresses around the world in the perpetual morning. The kitchen is the heart of the house, but nature is the kitchen of the world. However you slice it, this planetary Mother is our home. Native Americans think of the world as the Sacred Mother manifesting in physical form. But as we shall see, she is actually one half of divinity, the feminine complement to the Father God. The power of our kitchen work can be felt even more deeply if we learn more about the Mother God.

The concept of the Divine Mother is essential to many religions and traditions around the world. Hindus identify her manifestations as the goddesses Kali, Shakti, Parvati, Durga, and many others. The Tao is often described in feminine terms, such as the "Mother of all things." This is the philosophy that divides the entire universe into masculine and feminine counterparts: yin and yang. While classical Buddhism is essentially nondeist, Chinese Buddhism honors Quan Yin, the Goddess of Mercy. Mahayana Buddhism acknowledges the Mother of the Buddhas (Prajnaparamita), while Tantric Buddhism is well known for the importance it places on feminine principles in its practices.

The Book of Genesis tells us that God created the earth, and the pre-Olympian Greeks gave her a name: Gaia. Modern Gaia theory, first espoused by British chemist James E. Lovelock, asks us to believe that our planet is not just some empty-headed watery ball with a molten core, but a grand spiritual intelligence whose mind includes the ecosystems, atmosphere, oceans, and lands. She is the perpetual caretaker of all of life by continually adapting her own efficiency. Gaia is the World Mother, a working mother from whom everything we need for life grows freely and, with or without aggressive interference from us, pours forth abundantly. Such is the role of the cook within a household.

The pre-Judeo-Christian traditions are replete with feminine deities of every description. However, a return to worshipping goddesses is not necessary in order to acknowledge that in our sacred kitchens, the work we do makes us participants in God's feminine aspect. God, after all, is a Mother as well as a Father. It says so in Genesis, twice (authors' italics):

> So God created man in his [own] image, in the image of God created he him; *male and female created he them.*
>
> (Genesis 1:27)

> This [is] the book of the generations of Adam. In the day that God created man, in the likeness of God made he him; *Male and female created he them; and blessed them, and called their name Adam,* in the day when they were created.
>
> (Genesis 5:1-2)

Through scripture, we can embrace the divine masculine along with the divine feminine, guilt-free, and let the kitchen be Her temple in the home. With the power of God in your mind and heart when you cook, you are wielding some aspect of true kitchen power whether you are sweating over a mound of bread dough or opening a can electrically.

Mother Nature has her moods, but she always provides. When humankind hungers, in most places on earth they need only to reach up and grab a piece of fruit or swing a sickle for an armful of grain. Unless we live in a hostile place, or a place of drought or other catastrophe, we can pull radishes, carrots, and potatoes from out of the ground, and never have to go hungry. The Divine Mother must be very proud of Her earthly daughter, Mother Nature. She maintains annexes for Her beneficent jurisdiction in every household, right in the kitchen. The hands that feed the hungry mouths there belong to her representatives whenever cooking is done.

But there's more. From Her bounty comes not only food, but medicines. The plants used by shamans, medicine men and women, and herbalists for thousands of years to heal the sick are processed in modern times by pharmaceutical companies into expensive pills. Only 3 percent of Her pharmacopoeia has been researched, yet Her shelves grow empty as the rain forests, prime

sun, the farmers, the transporters, the market men and women, and the cooks who made it possible for it to be brought before us. We also give thanks for the company of those sharing the meal with us. We should sit with good posture and breathe deeply and calmly to facilitate digestion. Having acknowledged its source and prepared our body and mind for receiving it, with calm and glad heart, we enjoy our meal and renew ourselves.

— Cecile Tovah Levin, *Cooking for Regeneration*

sources for plant-based medicines, are destroyed. Pity the earth's children who may never know an important medicine because the only plant sources have been destroyed in the name of development.

"The earth is our ultimate nourishing organism," writes Sensei Shigeru Kanai, a Japanese Buddhist priest of the Butsungenshyu sect, in his book *The Path to Self-Healing: Sotaiho*. "Nature's elements produce wholesome foods, and when we eat food that is closer to these elements, more of nature's powerful energy will be passed on to us. . . .

"We can rekindle our connection to food as a Ceremony of Life, for this is linked with Mother Earth herself. For some of us, this connection is direct and heartfelt, and for those who would like to reconnect, it is very simple. The body, mind, and spirit respond quickly to foods which are nurturing and healing, therefore it is wise to eat foods which are pure and wholesome so that we may become whole ourselves."

From the energy of the life force in the universe to the chi flowing in your body, house, and kitchen, you play the role of Divine Mother in your sacred kitchen whenever you cook. If you think this way whenever you enter your kitchen, it can help you feel the life force in all the foods you are preparing, feel your connection to the global kitchen, and to the Father-Mother God.

The next time you're sipping your coffee, therefore, and before you read the paper, take a good look at your kitchen. Is it a worthy annex for the Divine Mother? Does it make you feel the power of the global kitchen? Is it a fine-tuned amplifier of the life force? Is there beauty, holiness, and power present there? Whether you sense the potential of your kitchen or cannot stop laughing at its current limitations, the feel of a temple can be revealed or created by examining the space itself to see what you can do to feel nearer to the sacred.

HOME IS WHERE THE HEARTH IS

The physical space of a kitchen plays an important role in your mood while you cook. So, before we look more deeply into the mystical, alchemical process of putting dinner on the table, let's look at your kitchen's design and how planetary chi flows through it.

Whether one uses a cast-iron pot hung from a hook over an open fire, an earthen bake oven, a wood-burning stove, or a "self-cleaning" range, one tries to make the tasks of cooking as convenient as possible. People keep the most often used foods and implements handy, while storing less-used ingredients and utensils in a cupboard, larder, pantry, or hanging from a tree — out of the reach of predators. It's a matter of logic and convenience.

On the Serengeti Plain, a community oven is intentionally placed downwind of the dwellings, convenient to the cooks and nearest to the river. Likewise, a fireplace is centrally located in a cabin so it can be used for heat as well as for cooking. Sometimes, however, modern kitchens aren't designed with the horse sense to make everything convenient, let alone a joy to work in.

This point is expressed beautifully in the book, *A Taste of Heaven: Adventures in Food and Faith*. Co-authors Rabbi Lionel Blue and June Rose write, "It is a pity so many kitchens today have modeled themselves on laboratories rather than on churches. Their gleaming whiteness can, I suppose, recall the purity and simplicity of a mosque. Usually all they recall is an atomic plant, or the outpatients ward at the local hospital. Kitchens are better when they are not only efficient in a mechanical way, but also efficient in a psychic and spiritual way, when they cater not only for the digestion of diners, but also for the soul of the cook, and all who pop in to visit. Like churches or chapels, they need some light and shade, some loved objects like old well-scrubbed tables, and some corners with unexpected treasures."

A kitchen should be designed and placed with some architectural and practical wisdom, not just as an afterthought in the space left over after the bedrooms and TV room have been designed. Stove, sink, and refrigerator should be in close proximity. Even if your appliances operate on a built-in computerized push-button system, the true home in your house is where the hearth — the kitchen — is.

In his book, *The Hungry Soul*, Leon R. Kass, M.D, writes: "Especially because modern times hold us hostage to the artificial

> The very spot where grew
> the bread
> That formed my bones,
> I see.
> How strange, old field,
> on thee to tread
> And feel I'm part of thee.
>
> — Abraham Lincoln

and the 'unreal,' we do well to remember that the hearth still makes the home, prepared and shared meals still make for genuine family life, and entertaining guests at dinner still nurtures the growth of friendship. A blessing offered over the meal still fosters a fitting attitude toward the world, whose gracious bounty is available to us and not because we merit it."

Anyone can tell you that harmony in the home is desirable, but in your kitchen, where you are turning nature's life force into dinner, some special touches are in order to tap even more hidden energies and harmonizing principles. In particular, we can utilize the ancient Chinese art of placement: *feng shui* (pronounced fung *shway*). Meaning "wind" and "water," feng shui is based on principles of design, mysticism, ecology, and architecture, with a healthy dose of common sense. It can be used to determine the best layout of a city or a building, as well as the placement of furniture within a room.

GOING WITH THE FLOW

Is your kitchen the kind of place where people like to congregate? Do you feel comfortable there? Or is it a place where you'd rather not spend any more time than necessary?

Denise Linn is an author, healer, and practitioner of "interior realignment" who believes that every item and space in a home has its attendant energy. In her book *Sacred Space*, she writes: "Your home is not just a composite of materials thrown together for shelter and comfort. Every cubic centimeter, whether solid or seemingly empty space, is filled with infinite vibrating energy fields. There are vast undulating patterns of energy fields overlapping within it and around it. There are a multitude of realms within your home. In addition to the purely physical realm of your home's structure and the physical objects within it, there are emotional energies and a multitude of spiritual and etheric energies constantly moving and swirling within your home."

Whether you know it or not, the chi flow in your kitchen may have everything to do with how it "feels" to be there. Through the

> The secret of seeking the will of God lies in cultivating the faculty of sensing harmony; for harmony is beauty and beauty is harmony, and the lover of beauty in his further progress becomes the seeker of harmony; and by trying always to maintain harmony, man will tune his heart to the will of God.
>
> — aphorisms from
> *The Sufi Message*,
> Hazrat Inayat Khan

use of feng shui, you can learn to enhance chi and achieve maximum harmony with the natural order.

Chi flow is one of the most important concepts in feng shui, and balancing and cultivating good chi is one of its primary aims. A feng shui practitioner will seek to create a balanced energy in a house. To aid in this balancing, there are a number of "cures," or remedies, that can be used to ensure positive chi flow and neutralize negative situations. For example, if a house has three or more doors or windows aligned in a row, the chi will be funneled through the house too quickly. A possible remedy to moderate this would be a wind chime strategically hung in the center window. In the instance of a dark and narrow hall, lights and mirrors may be used to symbolically open up the area to the flow of chi.

The central diagnostic tool of feng shui used for determining the placement of objects is the *bagua* (Figure 2.1), an eight-sided symbol from the *I Ching*. The eight sections are divided into departments of life: fame, marriage, children, benefactors, career, knowledge, family/health, and wealth. To put it to use, a bagua is superimposed over the floor plan of a house or a room in the house, with "career" along the front entrance wall. The bagua then becomes a guide for interpreting a person's life situations, correcting his or her limitations, or enhancing blessings. Simply put, a person who wants to improve his or her finances would implement "cures" to enhance the "wealth area" of the home.

The Bagua

The bagua correlates the physical spaces of a house to eight departments of life.

Figure 2.1

Inset: The bagua can be superimposed over a house or a room. Even in your kitchen, career is reflected along the entry wall, and fame on the farthest wall.

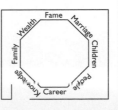

For there is not a member in the human body that does not have its counterpart in the world as a whole. For as man's body consists of members and parts of various ranks . . . so does the world at large consist of a hierarchy of created things, which when they properly act and react upon each other form literally one organic body.

—The Zohar

All told, there are a number of basic cures used to adjust, moderate, or raise the chi in an area of a room or home:

- Mirrors or other reflective objects
- Wind chimes or other objects that make pleasant sounds
- Plants or other living things, such as fish in an aquarium
- Water fountains or objects with a circular movement
- Statuary or other heavy objects
- Bamboo flutes or other long, hollow objects
- Colors, especially when used in a harmonious way

In each case, the cure affects the amount of chi or flow of chi through an area. Mirrors and water bring chi into a space that lacks it. Colors, plants, and sound soften or bend chi, while water is a powerful source of chi in and of itself.

KITCHEN FENG SHUI

In the kitchen, the most important factor is placement of the stove. This is because the stove is the symbolic source of wealth: All the food is cooked there. The Chinese word for food is *tsai,* which sounds similar to their word for wealth.

As Lin Yun, a leading feng shui master, puts it in Sarah Rossbach's book, *Feng Shui: The Chinese Art of Placement,* "From our food comes health and effectiveness. If it is well prepared and of good quality, we will do well in the world, earn more money to buy even better food." Conversely, he adds, "If you are poor, you eat worse, then fare poorly in the world." It is no coincidence that poor people in the U.S. eat a high percentage of junk food. Neither is it an accident that good-quality food is expensive, that is, unless you grow it yourself. Hence, the problem of a bad diet compounds the plight of the inner cities.

A kitchen with excellent chi flow is illustrated in Figure 2.2. The stove is placed in such a way that it allows the cook room to work. If it were placed in a cramped corner, this would inhibit the cook's chi. When this is the case, a mirror may be hung on the wall behind the stove to visually extend the space. Other kitchen hazards are angles of countertops, for example, which point at the cook. A possible cure would be to drape a viney plant down over the edge to soften it.

The most favorable stove site is one in which the cook can see all who enter the kitchen, thus allowing for smooth interaction. The theory is that if a cook faces away from the doorway, then health, wealth, and domestic harmony can be adversely affected. The cook's chi will be dispersed due to being startled by those entering the kitchen. Since most of us do not have the luxury of relocating our stove to a new position, a simple remedy is to, again, place a mirror behind the stove so the cook can see anyone entering the kitchen. You can also hang a wind chime near the door so a person entering brushes against it.

A Kitchen with Favorable Chi Flow

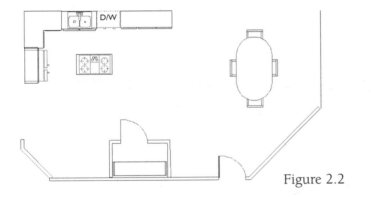

Figure 2.2

Figure 2.2 shows the position of the stove as beneficial, because it allows the cook to see anyone entering the kitchen. Also, the island stove provides an open, flowing arrangement.

The kitchen in Figure 2.2 shows a kitchen that has good chi flow, with furniture and appliances in favorable positions. Figure 2.3 shows a kitchen with blocked chi. The stove is crammed into a corner at the end of the room opposite the doorway. There is also a cabinet that is situated as to point sharp angles at the cook. Figure 2.4 shows how to remedy the obstructions through the use of mirrors, plants, and a wind chime or small crystal ball to activate more favorable chi.

It is interesting to note that in feng shui, the concept of yin

> The Taoist practice of chi cultivation focuses on integrating the divine or subtle energies into the human body, with the goal of achieving a dynamic balance of opposing energies called yin and yang. The Tao is the indescribable sum and absolute source of these energies, which manifest in ever changing form.
>
> — Mantak Chia and Michael Winn, *Taoist Secrets of Love*

Feng Shui Problems and Cures

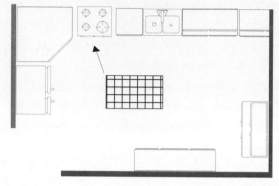

Figure 2.3

Figure 2.3 shows a kitchen with feng shui problems. The stove is poorly placed and cramped. The cook is unable to see people entering the kitchen. The corner of the island counter points at the cook.

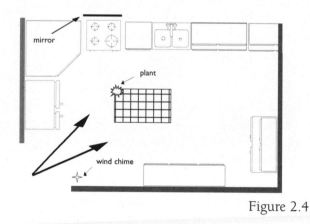

Figure 2.4

Figure 2.4 shows the kitchen from Figure 2.3 with following feng shui cures: A wind chime has been hung near the door for harmonious flow of chi; a mirror has been installed over the stove to reveal visitors; a plant has been placed on the corner of the center island to soften the sharp edge pointing at the cook.

and yang energies are employed to bring about balance and harmony in your surroundings. These same yin and yang principles are the foundation of Taoism, as well as important elements of balance in diet that we examine more closely in chapter 4.

In addition to employing the precepts of feng shui, there are other nuances that can greatly add to the harmony of your kitchen. Keep your kitchen well lit and ventilated. Keep it clean, with the equipment in good working order. Incorporate green plants or fresh flowers into the decor to add life force to your surroundings and improve the quality of the air. And display a bowl of fresh organic fruits or vegetables so that the life force of your food is not confined to the pantry or refrigerator.

Place some familiar objects in the room that add warmth to the environment, helping to make your kitchen more homey and less sterile. Western kitchens seem to imitate the ambiance of institutional settings, in which, except for designer colors and cabinet doors, surfaces are plain and the decor is practical. A few obligatory "kitcheny" icons are usually placed here and there such as decorator trivets and pictures of chickens, vegetables, or flowers, with matching dish towels — often with no real thought or meaning other than to "decorate."

Now is the time to get out your grandmother's antique rolling pin, coffee grinder, or favorite lace tablecloth. You can buy a few old kitchen implements at an antique shop or flea market, and they can add a connection to the past. An old or old-looking clay pot or figure can help remind you of our primordial connection to the World Mother. A small sheaf of dried wheat tied with twine would be a symbol of her generosity. All of these ideas can help family and guests feel connected to the Creator of all life, as well as to each other and the world in the global kitchen.

You can burn candles in your sacred kitchen or display symbols of your religious faith. Wear clothing made of natural fibers, not just while you cook, but anytime. Simple touches like these can greatly contribute to a harmonious atmosphere. You will discover that the happier you are, and the more free from stress, the better your food will be. Your kitchen can become your haven. Your temple.

> I have three chairs in my house: one for solitude, two for friendship, and three for society.
>
> — Henry David Thoreau

A drop in the ocean partakes of the greatness of its parent although it is unconscious of it. But it is dried up as soon as it enters upon an existence independent of the ocean.

— Mahatma Gandhi

Consider listening to peaceful, soothing music when you work in your kitchen. The delicate strains of a Bach concerto can do wonders for your spirits as well as for the lasagna. It will help you come out of the kitchen refreshed and humming instead of grouchy and grumbling.

Based on the foregoing, here is a list of ten simple things you can do to enhance your sacred cooking space, short of an all-out remodeling job:

- Use feng shui items such as mirrors and crystals for harmonious chi flow.
- Maintain good lighting.
- Have adequate ventilation.
- Use green plants and other natural objects to promote chi and add natural beauty.
- Keep kitchen surfaces clean and tidy.
- Keep appliances clean and in good repair.
- Display familiar objects such as antiques and cheerful pictures to add warmth.
- Decorate with pleasing colors and textures, including handmade objects.
- Place personal sacred symbols where you can see them.
- Play peaceful, soothing music.

These additions and changes will not only add to the visual appeal of your kitchen, but will help to convey a spiritual feeling. The goal is to make the kitchen a joy to be in, a place that regenerates and heals you because of the sacred activity you do there: cooking.

Due to its function alone, the kitchen is the heart of the house. But as you reorient the chi flow in your sacred kitchen and thereby in your home, remember to attend to the energy needs of the other rooms. Apply the principles of feng shui to the building as a whole and then to each room. Let the function of each room be clear, and let the activities there connect in your consciousness in some way to the Creator. This will help give your kitchen a sacred identity in your home.

Sacred Space author Denise Linn writes, "Our homes are mirrors of ourselves. They reflect our interests, our beliefs, our hesitations, our spirit, and our passion. They tell a story about how we feel about ourselves and the world around us. A home is more than a place to lay your head and seek comfort from the elements. It is a place where you can interface with the universe. It is a crossing point in time and space that can attract energy or repel energy."

With this background on the far-reaching implications of fixing a bite to eat, it's time to take steps to change the way you think about yourself in your kitchen. You can do this by finding the sacred space within you called your "center." The center is a state of mind in which you are able to feel close to God and closer to the souls who come to your kitchen to eat. In the next chapter we explain how to explore your centeredness, and in chapter 4, the centeredness of food. Once you prepare your outer space, the space in which you cook, you can then turn inward and prepare mentally and emotionally to find the sacred within.

RECIPES FOR BALANCE IN THE SENSES

The following recipes are designed to promote balance in all the senses, mirroring the harmony you create in your kitchen through a pleasing visual appeal and delicious aromas and flavors.

During the preparation of these recipes, be mindful of the beauty of the ingredients you are preparing: their color, fragrance, texture. Feel the cool water on your hands as you cleanse each leaf; listen to the sound as your knife cuts into the ginger and releases its pungent aroma. Let it tickle your nose, as you remember how every ingredient is a gift from the Divine Mother.

Prepared with these ideas in mind, this simple meal of soup and rice, combined with the creamy richness of the berry pudding, may be one of the most satisfying you have ever had.

ECSTASY JADE SOUP

A harmonious blending of textures and flavors combine in a delicate yet pungent soup. The watercress provides a lovely healing green color. Serve this soup in pure white bowls.

10 ounces firm silken tofu, cut into $1/4$-inch dice
1 tablespoon plus 1 teaspoon canola oil
$3/4$ teaspoon cornstarch
$1/4$ teaspoon salt
$1/8$ teaspoon cayenne pepper
4 cups Vital Vegetable Stock (page 172)
2 thin slices fresh ginger
8 ounces fresh watercress, stemmed
   (4 sprigs reserved for garnish)
1 tablespoon tamari sauce
1 teaspoon sake or dry white wine
1 teaspoon toasted sesame oil

In a small bowl, combine the tofu with the 1 teaspoon canola oil, the cornstarch, salt, and cayenne. Refrigerate for 30 minutes.

Bring the stock and ginger to a boil in a medium saucepan. Add the watercress and tamari. Boil for 3 minutes. Reduce heat to low.

Heat the 1 tablespoon canola oil in a large saucepan or wok over medium-high heat. Add the tofu mixture and stir for 1 minute. Add the sake or wine, stock mixture, and sesame oil. Cook for 2 minutes. Transfer the soup to bowls, discarding the ginger. Garnish each with a sprig of watercress.

Serves 4

Golden Sun Sauté

Radiant with the colors of the sun, this healthful sauté is a feast for the senses.

1 tablespoon canola oil
1 small yellow onion, halved lengthwise and thinly
   sliced
1 tablespoon grated fresh ginger
2 garlic cloves, minced
1 yellow bell pepper, seeded, deribbed, and cut into
   thin strips
$1/2$ red bell pepper, seeded, deribbed, and cut into thin
   strips
2 teaspoons Madras curry powder
1 large carrot, grated
1 yellow summer squash, cut into $1/4$-inch rounds
2 tablespoons or more tamari sauce
1 teaspoon packed light brown sugar (optional)
4 cups Brown Rice with Love (page 21)
$1/2$ cup golden raisins
$1/2$ cup cashew nuts

Heat the oil in a large skillet or wok over medium-high heat. Add the onion, ginger, and garlic and stir-fry for 2 minutes. Add the bell peppers and stir-fry until almost tender, about 2 minutes. Add the curry powder, carrot, and squash and stir-fry for 2 minutes. Add the tamari and brown sugar (if using) and stir-fry for 30 seconds, or until well combined. Spoon a bed of rice on each dinner plate and top with a portion of the vegetable mixture. Garnish each serving with the raisins and cashews.

Serves 4

It is clear to me that unless we connect directly with the earth, we will not have the faintest clue why we should save it. We need to have dirt under our fingernails and to experience that deep aching sense of physical tiredness after a day's labor in the garden to really understand nature.

— Helen Caldicott, M.D.,
If You Love This Planet

SAMADHI-LOVES-YOU BANANA-BERRY PUDDING

To Buddhists and Hindus, *samadhi* ("total self-collectiveness") is a state of rapture achieved through meditation and concentration and is the climax of all spiritual and intellectual activity. The exquisite taste of this pudding can be a rapturous experience.

3 cups fresh strawberries, hulled and halved
$1/4$ cup sugar or a natural sweetener
$1/2$ cup firm silken tofu, blotted
1 banana, quartered
$1/2$ teaspoon fresh lemon juice
Pinch of salt
Fresh mint sprigs for garnish

Put the strawberries in a blender or food processor, pulsing to form a puree. Add the sugar or other sweetener, tofu, banana, lemon juice, and salt and process until thoroughly mixed. Transfer to dessert dishes. Refrigerate for at least 2 hours. Serve garnished with mint sprigs.

Serves 4 to 6

A Hindu Mealtime Blessing

O God, bless this food so that it brings vitality and energy to fulfill
Thy mission and serve humanity.
O God, bless this food so that we remain aware of Thee within and without.
O God, bless this food so that we love all and exclude none.
Bless those who have provided this food, who have prepared
this food and who will eat this food. Bless all, my Lord. Amen.

We praise You, Eternal God, Sovereign of the universe, for You cause bread to come forth from the earth.

— *ha-motzi, the Jewish blessing for bread*

3

Self-Help with Salt and Pepper

If there is harmony in the house,
There will be order in the nation.
If there is order in the nation,
There will be peace in the world.

— Chinese proverb

Now that your kitchen has been remedied for maximum chi flow, it's time to work on your own chi. After all, once you've taken every step to create a sacred atmosphere, if you have never felt sacredness within yourself, all you've really done is redecorate. As the cook, you too are holy, and this chapter will show you how to find that holiness. The secret is to find a space within your consciousness where you can relax and recharge whenever you wish — a place of transcendent beauty. Give these techniques some practice, and once inside your centeredness, even washing the dishes will make you feel simply divine.

THE STRESS FACTOR

To get started finding that centeredness within, all you need to do is free yourself from the tyranny of stress. But that's not so easy, is it? Or is it?

Stress became a household word during the 1980s, when it was declared a medical condition with specific effects on job performance, home life, temperament, and mental and physical health. Since stress weakens the immune system, it is now believed that 50 to 80 percent of all illness is stress related. Over 40 million Americans take medication to battle the symptoms of stress. If you feel older than you should, have no energy, feel depressed, anxious, exhausted, lacking in motivation, and plain lousy every day, you may be stressed out.

You know you've been there: excited to have a new job; struggling to make an impression; devastated by some costly mistake. Others are competing, and the playing field is uneven. You are given the work of two people, but quality cannot suffer. There isn't time for it all. And then there's your home life. If you run a household, especially with children, you know the routine. You have a new gas grill in the backyard that you haven't used and two-week-old magazines unread. Pressures mount, and pretty soon your whole nervous system is occupied with the home, the office, troubled relationships, and fears. It's even difficult to relax when you are at play or on vacation.

We try to deal with stress by using a variety of healthy and unhealthy coping mechanisms: going to the gym, playing sports, engaging in hobbies, using alcohol and drugs, having or avoiding sex, and marrying our jobs. Some quit the rat race and move to the country, and many of us eat when we are stressed.

The Buddhists say the more fears and desires in our lives, the more frustrations and unhappiness. Meditation is the answer, they say: setting aside some time every day in which to be at peace, to be free from fear and desire, and to help you maintain overall mental and physical health.

Psychologists and medical doctors agree. Unrelieved tension can contribute to general poor health. In his book *Full Catastrophe*

A Dozen Stress Reducers You Can Count On

1. Regular exercise
2. Prayer and/or meditation
3. Long walks
4. Hot baths
5. Massage
6. Aromatherapy
7. Yoga
8. Tai chi
9. Managing your time by making lists
10. Painting, sculpting, and other arts
11. Adopting a pet
12. Eating a healthy diet

Living, Jon Kabat-Zinn, founder and director of the Stress Reduction Clinic at the University of Massachusetts Medical Center, gives dozens of case stories of chronically ill patients who transformed themselves physically, mentally, and emotionally through meditation practices. These transformations manifested as significant reductions of symptoms, elimination of pain, and improvements in the quality of their lives.

Kabat-Zinn says that we expect medicine to fix anything that goes wrong with us, but it is increasingly recognized that "our active collaboration is essential in almost all forms of medical therapy."

He writes, "Taking responsibility for learning more about your own body by listening to it carefully and by cultivating your inner resources for healing and maintaining health is the best way to hold up your end of this collaboration with your doctors and with medicine. This is where the meditation practice comes in. It gives power and substance to such efforts. It catalyzes the work of healing."

How much better can meditation practice improve the lives of people who are free of chronic illness? In *Natural Health, Natural Medicine*, Andrew Weil, M.D., reports on the medical evidence for the benefits of meditation. "Researchers documented immediate benefits in terms of lowered blood pressure, decreased heart and respiratory rate, increased blood flow, and other measurable signs of the relaxation response."

Weil reports that a regular meditation practice can:

- Calm an agitated mind
- Create optimal physical and mental health
- Undo our sense of separateness (source of fear and misery)
- Unify consciousness, putting us in touch with our higher self and connecting us through higher consciousness
- Restructure the mind, allowing us to achieve our full potential as human beings

So why doesn't everyone meditate? Bernie Siegel, M.D., the physician who brought the element of love to cancer medicine in his groundbreaking *Love, Medicine, and Miracles*, says "Relaxation and meditation are perhaps especially difficult for Americans. Our constant mental diet of advertising, noise, violence, and media stimulation makes it very difficult to endure even a few minutes of inactivity and quiet."

We can overcome these obstacles to finding our inner peace. Your willingness to try is the first step, and *The Sacred Kitchen* provides simple techniques for meditation as well as a higher-consciousness context to make it easier to adopt: Cooking is performing miracles with the life force, while linked to the global kitchen, in a sacred space deliberately intended for communing with the Divine. The idea is to get more out of cooking time than just fulfilling another responsibility. You can actually turn cooking into a focus for meditation. Whenever you cook, don't allow yourself to think about problems and concerns. Leave them outside the doorway to your sacred kitchen and be in the moment.

Learning to meditate is really not so difficult to do. After all, at least you don't have to cook dinner in a firehouse.

THE FIREFIGHTER'S STORY

Danny Lliteras, a firefighter in Norfolk, Virginia, is a genuine American hero. He demonstrates his heroism every day along with other firefighters across the nation. Despite the dangers, however, he doesn't consider his job stressful. He's been doing rescue work for many years: as a Marine corpsman in Vietnam during the 1960s and as a rescue and salvage diver for the U.S. Navy. But there's another type of stress that wears on any firefighter. Strangely, it's the stress of the firehouse itself.

There is constant noise. Horns and sirens. Hollering. Radio monitors blare out every call in the city. Alarm monitors go off as vehicles of all kinds depart and return around the clock. Other firefighters are living around you. There is no privacy at the station, and sleep is regularly interrupted.

When he's not risking his life out on a call, Lliteras is a firehouse cook. He loves it and actually uses cooking to transcend the stresses of firehouse life. Not only that, but he finds cooking to be a meditative activity.

"When I'm cooking, I've got complete focus," he says. "A firehouse cook doesn't do anything else but cook, and everybody leaves the cook alone. Except for responding to the calls with the rest of the fire company, he runs his own day. He has to plan the menus, do the shopping, peel the potatoes, and get the meals on the table. He's in and out of the galley and does what he wants to do." The rest of the company is occupied with other duties that should sound familiar to anyone who keeps house: cleaning, washing, polishing, vacuuming the floors, paperwork, and taking out the trash.

Lliteras is also an author who has written five novels with contemplative themes under the name D S Lliteras. As a writer, he appreciates the quiet niche his cooking job affords him.

"There's a certain sense of rhythm, particularly in the mornings," he says. "That's when I'm getting lunch ready or prepping for dinner. This will be when the guys are sitting around in the galley talking and not much is going on. There's a certain community sense, a sense of family."

"You try to plan meals that aren't so complex that they'll be ruined by a fire call," he adds. That limits the menu, but it stimulates creativity. "It can be irritating when you have two or three pots going, something in the oven, and 'the brass hits' — an alarm goes off."

Firehouse cooks serve meals that can be interrupted three or four times, whether for genuine calls or false alarms. "At that point, a lot of guys lose their appetites and just say 'forget it.'"

Being a firehouse cook protects Lliteras from other more routine duties during the slow hours between calls. He typically spends half of his shifts cooking breakfast, lunch, and dinner for anywhere from four to eight men, who wolf down every meal. "Firefighters are very fast eaters," he says. "They learn to gobble their food."

The noise, demands, and interruptions are a little like what a homemaker with a large family faces every day. But even in a smaller household, how often have you felt overwhelmed at dinnertime, having to cook dinner when you don't have time, with constant interruptions, and serving meals to preoccupied people who are in too much of a hurry?

Lliteras is a firefighter who actually uses cooking as a stress

> The Buddha said that the problem of life and death is itself the problem of mindfulness. Whether or not one is alive, depends on whether one is mindful.
>
> —Thich Nhat Hanh, *The Miracle of Mindfulness*

Those whose minds are well fixed upon the elements of enlightenment, who, without hankering after anything, glory in renunciation, whose biases are extinguished, who are full of light, they indeed have attained the bliss of Nirvana in this very world.

— Buddha,
The Dhammapada

reducer. While cooking, he finds peace and tranquillity amid the din. He attributes his cool handling of hot situations to his fire-fighting training and experience, but also to a meditation practice that he learned at Florida State University. As an acting student, he was taught techniques for "centering" himself and being in the "here and now" while performing — techniques he has used throughout his career.

These techniques opened the door to a new spiritual life for Lliteras during the late 1980s, when he picked up a copy of D. T. Suzuki's *What Is Zen?* for fifty cents at a used-books store. He has been practicing Zen-style meditation almost as long as he has been a firefighter. For him, meditation has become a way to mellow out, to develop the inner person, and reach out to a greater power — to God — in his life.

Once each morning, Lliteras sits in the traditional cross-legged *zazen* posture to prepare for his day. In his meditative state, he contacts the "center," that place of peace and perspective within that will serve him, no matter what frustrations the day may bring. Using his technique throughout the day, he can "shut down" when the little stuff starts getting to him. With meditation, he evens out the peaks and valleys of his life. He has been practicing meditation for so long, he can bring himself to that centeredness at will, to let disappointments and most troubles pass without disturbing it.

A meditation practice, whether formal or simple, can smooth the rough edges of our lives and teach us how to put things on "hold" — to deal with distractions and just *let things go*. This is because, while we can't change the world around us, we can change our reactions, our vulnerabilities, and the sensitivities of our precious egos. A meditation practice can allow us to find the calm center within whenever we need it, even if we never have to cook dinner in a firehouse.

Just as Suzuki's little book helped Danny Lliteras turn inward to seize control of his centeredness, we can all find the inspiration to look within and discover a peaceful haven. For some, it will be a book or a teaching, for others, a church, temple, mosque, or synagogue. For still others, it can be a life-or-death wake-up call.

Above all, don't rule out the possibility that you can find the inspiration you need in your sacred kitchen.

HEALING IN THE KITCHEN SINK

As we nurture the idea of creating a kitchen temple in the home, there's another temple that needs tending as well: the temple that is *you*. Just as your kitchen is the "holy of holies" in your house, your feeling heart is the "holy of holies" within you. This center is all-wise and all-loving: the very image of the Creator out of which we all came to be. The closer we can get to this holy of holies, the more centered we are in our consciousness. We can find this center and reduce the stress in our lives by learning a simple meditation practice and by adopting a holy attitude whenever we perform our kitchen duties.

You may be saying to yourself: "Even if I call it sacred when I'm making a peanut butter and jelly sandwich, kitchen work is still kitchen work." Yes, we still have to get out the jars, cans, produce, pots, pans, oil, utensils; make dinner; and then clean it up and put it all away. What's so darned sacred or joyful about this daily routine?

The monastics of many religions have the answer. The monks, yogis, and ascetics who spend so much time on bended knees, in prayer, scrubbing the floor of a grand portico with a toothbrush, weeding a forty-acre garden, or peeling a mountain of potatoes, see all labor as service to their religious ideal. Who else feels this grateful for lessons in patience, humility, or appreciation for the holiness of work itself? For them, the very simplicity of such a life is its own reward. But the simple virtues of their religious practices can help reveal to anyone the secret benefits of keeping a sacred kitchen. The secret is in training the mind. Without training, the mind is little more than a drunken monkey, or a mischievous puppy without a leash.

Buddhist masters teach a principle called "mindfulness," an essential ingredient to mental and physical health that's often lacking in Western life. Our energies are pulled in a dozen directions at once, but mindfulness can turn it around. If we can't create

Meditation brings stress
to its knees.

— K. R. S. Edstrom,
Conquering Stress

peace in the world around us, then surely we can find it within. Turn your kitchen into a sacred place and your kitchen work into a blessing rather than a burden, and you can create a safe haven within your home. Whether mopping the floor, closing a business deal, or shopping for a house, we all need to discipline our minds to be aware of our presence in the *now*.

Begin thinking of the kitchen as a temple. Turn cooking into a sacrament. Be a priest or priestess whenever you cook, free from fear and frustration. You can get to this place by introducing meditation, a healthy stress reducer into your daily routine.

"Wash the dishes to wash the dishes," writes Zen Buddhist monk Thich Nhat Hanh, "not for the cup of tea afterwards." But Hanh isn't alone in his advice for us preoccupied Westerners. Swami Satchidananda, founder of Integral Yoga International, teaches that the "golden present" is *all there is*. Since the past is gone and the future hasn't happened yet, our chance to heal our lives — to live our lives — exists only now, in this present that is full of unlimited opportunities. Living in the present, we can heal our lives and keep ourselves healthy. We can find solace in empty space, and healing in the kitchen sink. We can also find the center — the "sweet, creamy center" of our souls.

THE SWEET, CREAMY CENTER

A sweet, creamy center exists within all of us. It is the joyful stillness that monks of all religions strive for, and that can be found by practicing meditation. It is the experience of children during that brief window of time before they become filled with the concerns, fears, and doubts of the world.

When we were babies, the sweet, creamy center is all there was. It was who we were before we learned to doubt and worry. We can all remember as children, playing, inventing, and imagining our way through summer days; those endless days in which we didn't seek meaning in the universe: we were the universe. Certain special days ended in the magic of twilight, with fireflies and hot skin dewy from the urgency of kickball or watching the stars before it was time to come in.

In adult life, we occasionally find that sweet, creamy center again. We find it when we fall in love, joy bursting from our hearts in complete faith that the bumblebee of romance can really fly. Graduations, receiving honors, landing those hoped-for jobs, big raises — all such events transport us there for another brief taste. With the births of children, and through the vicarious triumphs we enjoy when our kids excel, we swell with sweetness. And it happens again when new friendships blossom, and on seeing a grand natural vista, and during those moments when Spirit reminds us in some personal way that we are loved from on high. Awesome coincidences or miraculous changes of fortune stir our I AM greatness, and in those moments we feel connected with the All, the sweet, creamy center in the heart of the universe.

We can see examples of centeredness in history and Scripture, in the prophets and patriarchs who knew God face to face. On Mt. Sinai, Moses received the name of God, I AM THAT I AM, from the bush that burned with fire but was not consumed. Before divine intervention, Daniel exhibited great centeredness in the lion's den where *he* was to be the dinner. Away from the world and in the presence of the Angel, Mohammed received the *suras* that would become the Holy Qu'ran. Centeredness in the storm was demonstrated by Jesus walking on the water. He also overcame the temptations of the world during forty days and nights in the desert. From Jesus' centeredness came forth teachings of perfect love and compassion.

Counselor, author, and speaker John Bradshaw showed us the sweet, creamy center in the "inner child" movement, in which people can find the child they had once been and heal childhood traumas by revisiting moments of abuse, injury, or their unfulfilled need for love. It's not heaven or nirvana. But the center of yourself, where you can be free from stress and regain moments of peace and innocence, even forgiveness and renewal, can be discovered and cultivated.

In order to find that center, we need to periodically escape the din around us and quiet the nagging noises and desires that tend to emerge from our daily routine. We can do this by training the mind to quiet itself each day with meditation. All the world's prophets, from Moses to Jesus, used quiet moments to help

> I felt it better to speak to God than about him.
>
> — St. Thérèse of Lisieux

**The Four Noble
Truths of Buddhism**

The Truth of Suffering
The Truth of Origin
The Truth of Cessation
The Truth of the Path

themselves hear the awesome voice of the Creator, apart from the madding crowd and even away from their closest friends. In the silence of meditation, we can find the sweet, creamy center again at will and remember that it's always there when we need it. Practice enough, and we can take inner peace along with us during the day. We can recharge, even when we make dinner.

There are many meditation systems taught around the world, and they are based on various traditions. Some of these systems are so complicated, they take years to learn. If you are too busy, or not inclined to commit to some new spiritual practice, you can still pick up these simple techniques for mental discipline and incorporate them into your routine whatever your religion or belief system may be.

Like clearing the table after dinner, meditation is a simple way to periodically clear your mind. This tool can be a real buddy. It only requires four elements:

1. Choose a quiet, comfortable place in which to meditate. A porch, balcony, broom closet, or any personal space with a closeable door will do. You can be seated in a chair or on the floor. Be comfortable, but avoid lying down, as falling asleep is not the goal.

2. Be aware and in control of your breathing. To begin, close your eyes. Inhale deeply through the nose and then slowly exhale through the mouth. On the in-breath, visualize incoming white light permeating and surrounding your being. On the out-breath, release negative thoughts, fears, and emotional baggage as if they are smoke. First fill your belly, then your chest, and then fill your lungs up under your shoulders. This is called a "yogic breath," and it gives you 20 percent more air and *prana* (the Indian word for chi) than ordinary breathing. It really works. Change the rate and depth of your breathing, and you can calm any negative mood in three breaths.

3. Enjoy a sustained oasis in the silence. Your success at achieving stillness will come gradually. When thoughts intrude, let them pass like clouds across the sky. Be the observer, and don't let the thoughts engage you or take you away with them. Don't let them lead you away, but just let them go, whatever they are. The peaceful spaces *in between these thoughts* will gradually widen and lengthen with practice. Strive to extend the peaceful experience for two to three minutes. With diligence, some people will see results within a day or so. Others may require more time.

4. Practice regularly. Regular practice is vital, even taking three minutes in the morning, afternoon, and evening. Strive for at least one five- to ten-minute meditation per day. Regard these quiet times as your special opportunities to bask in this peaceful place in your heart — the place that is close to the center of you, close to the Creator's I AM within you.

If you can sit in a quiet place where you won't be disturbed for two or three minutes and be still in your mind and body, this can help you conquer stress and move closer to your center. You can add to the practice as much as you wish and custom fit it for your needs. Use this simple method for all the meditation exercises in this book.

Here are some ways to add sanctity to your meditations, energize your body, and share your newfound holiness with others:

• Choose your favorite prayers to open and close the session. In the middle of your experience, use a special prayer, one that makes you feel holy, grateful, healed. Thank the Creator for everything you have, however you define God for yourself. These precious moments, apart from the outside world of demands and the inside world of thoughts and feelings, will begin to make a home within you and provide a new foundation for your day.

• As you breathe, visualize the white light flowing down through the top of your head, in, through, and around every part of your body, cell, nerve, organ, from head to foot. Imagine a warm, healing effect during your long, controlled breaths. Pray for others — there is no better way to free yourself from self-

> Behold, I stand before the door, and knock: if any man hear my voice, and open the door, I will come in to Him, and will sup with Him, and He with me.
>
> — The Revelation of Saint John, 3:20

If your mind is empty, it is
always ready for
anything; it is open to
everything. In the
beginner's mind
there are many
possibilities; in the expert's
mind
there are few.

— Shunryu Suzuki,
Zen Mind, Beginner's Mind

preoccupying thoughts than to bestow benefits on others, directly or indirectly. That's the sweet, creamy center that encourages people to give back to you.

• When you are facing a tough problem in your life, before you meditate, ask to receive guidance. By finding centeredness, your decisions won't be influenced by either an outcome you fear or a particular one to which you are especially attached. During the meditation or during the day or week ahead, the divine light will come through, and with patience you will receive the solution.

• Would you like to improve your relationships with others? Once you've found your own center you can be much more relaxed in the world knowing that everyone possesses this holy place within. Getting through the day is easier when you honor the center in others — even when they are being nasty in your face.

With practice, something very important can happen from regular meditation. Eventually, the breath alone will bring on a feeling of peace. This will help you return to the sweet, creamy center even when you don't have time to go off by yourself. Traffic jam? Business meeting? Bad news from your child's principal? Not a problem. You know there is a universal space — a consciousness throughout the universe that isn't afraid or worried, and you can go there any time you wish, yes, even while you prepare dinner. Breathe with the in-breath and out-breath of Creation itself. You will tend to get calmer between your meditation sessions. It will help you make better decisions, because those decisions won't be based on frenetic mental activity distorted by stress.

Varanasi Kabir was a fifteenth-century Indian mystic and poet who tried to unite Hindus and Muslims. He preached the essential unity of all faiths and the intrinsic equality of all people. His student, Nanak, established the religion of Sikhism. "Don't go outside to see the flowers," wrote Kabir. "My friend, don't bother with that journey. Inside your body there are many flowers. One flower has a thousand petals, and that will do for a place to sit. Sitting there you can glimpse the beauty inside the body and out of it, before gardens and after gardens."

The Indian mystic uses a garden paradise from the outside world as a symbol for the inner world, a perfect example of how to use meditation to bring the sacred kitchen alive. In the garden of the mind, you want to clear the weeds of worry, discontent, and stress, and in the resulting centeredness plant seeds of peace and beauty that you will enjoy visiting often. Within your home, you want to think of your kitchen as the centered haven in which you are aware of your holiness as well as of the divinity of the life force with which you are working. Centeredness in the universe, within your house, and within you — they are all connected when you cook.

For the authors, applying meditation in the sacred kitchen begins in their backyard.

THE HEALING GARDEN

The principles that we have written down in this book actually began in our garden, which continues to renew our excitement and commitment to our sacred kitchen every spring.

In 1992, when we bought our fifty-year-old house, a wise nurserywoman told us to hold back on planting for a season so we wouldn't destroy existing perennials that hadn't sprouted yet. She was right. Each successive season, new shoots and blooms amazed us like found gold: beauty we didn't have to pay for because it "came with the place." Over time, we've noted the locations of dozens of old seasonals and now enjoy all the creative ideas of previous owners.

We have always loved fresh vegetables, but our landscape design only accommodates a small herb garden in one corner. After that first year, we couldn't wait to get started on our herb garden. We sacrificed a stand of unhealthy cannas that occupied the corner and dug it out, root by root. We were just beginners as gardeners, but we soon got lost in the planning and the digging, feeling the energy of the earth as it wedged under our fingernails. We put a small stone lantern in the center of the new space and consecrated the spot where the herbs would grow. The exercise of that first garden turned into a meditation that lasted all morning. In the

The Six Perfections of Buddhism

Generosity

Ethics

Patience

Effort

Concentration

Wisdom

Silence is the garden of
meditation.

— Ali, *Maxims of Ali*

afternoon, we went to the nursery and went wild buying herb plants of every kind.

We planted sweet basil to ensure a continuous supply of fresh pesto sauce. Then we surrounded the stone lantern with oregano for our homemade vegan pizzas, and parsley, tarragon, chives, mint, rosemary, and lemon balm to adorn salads all summer long. The garden work stretched over weeks, drawing us back to its meditative hug each day after work.

Even though we had dug up every inch of ground to get rid of the cannas, some stowaway morning glories still grow every year, coiling sensuously up the shafts of two bamboo torches. The morning blooms seem to trumpet a silent fanfare in honor of the herbs. In the center of our garden a showy red-leafed tropical plant grows — it's an old planting that also eluded the spade. We don't know what it is, but by mid-July it's the centerpiece of the garden. Over six years later, the little herb garden is our pride and joy. We've even managed to include a few vegetable plants between the azaleas and gardenias. By August, we enjoy tomatoes, peppers, summer squash, and cucumbers.

Spring comes early in southeastern Virginia, usually on the heels of a mild, snowless winter. As soon as the threat of frost passes, we suspend all writing and go outside to turn over the garden. We weed, rake, spade, and fertilize, and somehow the work draws us back into that sweet, creamy center inside us where the inner child comes out to play. Worries and concerns are gone, no plans occupy our thoughts, and we are mindful of only the task at hand. We are in the moment as we buy our herbs, along with colorful flowers such as begonias and impatiens to plant at the edges of the beds. Trowels in hand, we dig, plant, pack, and water each plant.

Only then do we turn our attention to the rest of the yard. We rake up winter's leavings of pine straw, cones, and leaves and freshen up the beds of roses, hydrangea, azaleas, gardenias, nandina, hibiscus, juniper, and hosta. As we work in the garden, we laugh at the new spring children of cardinals and blue jays as well as the neighborhood doves, grackles, chickadees, and finches that demand seeds from us on a constant basis. We scold them and complain as we fill and refill the feeders. Since we live near the beach, we also observe the seagulls and an occasional blue heron or snowy egret flying high overhead.

The little herb garden continues to be a meditation for us through the summer: weeding, aerating, and fertilizing the soil, yes, but especially picking the redolent leaves every day just before dinner. For us, the garden has become a yoga, a discipline of mind and body: hand and knee work that's so good for the soul.

Thinking of our garden work in this way doesn't take the fun out of it. We just go with the flow and release other responsibilities for a time. Planting and cultivating the garden is completely stress free. From the first spade turn of spring, we feel so close to the life force — the chi — of the earth.

With our desire for fresh sauces and salads, we begin to infuse love into the food these herbs will grace six weeks hence. This is an extension of the powers of the heart and hands described in chapter 1. We begin to impart our energy into the food we eat even before we plant it, then continually as it grows, as we harvest it and finally as we serve it.

The garden meditation thus becomes a kitchen meditation. We begin picking sprigs of tarragon and rosemary to try on seitan roasts or to complement potatoes and salad. We begin topping the basil plants glowing with fresh life force and with them make our beloved pesto. The sweet, heady leaves are bursting with aroma just from the picking, but then they are ground with garlic, pine nuts, and olive oil in the mortar (or food processor, when time is short) to make the famous bright green Italian sauce. Our sacred kitchen fills with the redolence of food made fresh from the Divine Mother's abundance. From the heart of the kitchen, the aroma flows throughout the body of the house. Such labor does not have to be thought of as mundane, for it is mystical. A miracle. It's not farming, but prayer. Not yard chores, but yoga. Not making dinner, but alchemy. The alchemy that takes nature's holy energy, and transforms it with love into energy that enables our bodies to live.

In the late afternoon, the morning glories rest from their dawn vigil as we eat the vibrantly fresh food at our umbrella-covered patio table that overlooks the garden. We munch fresh grilled fennel bulbs, tomatoes with basil, and dilled cucumbers — with just

> Whether you tend a garden or not, you are the gardener of your own being, the seed of your destiny.
>
> — David Spangler,
> Afterword to *The Findhorn Garden*

a dash of salt and pepper. We recall every step, from the planting of the herbs to the preparation and cooking. Every bite is synchronized with the dinner being prepared perpetually in the global kitchen. With only a little space, or even a window box in a city high-rise, anyone can touch and taste the beauty of living herbs and make their kitchen and food that much more sacred.

You can use anything as a focus for meditation — even nothing! But various activities, aside from cooking and gardening, can be used. Many people meditate without realizing it. People can find themselves lulled into a meditative state while riding a bicycle or washing windows. Apply the meditation techniques above to any activity, and it will make it easier to apply it in your sacred kitchen when you cook.

Whether you risk your life putting out real fires or only figurative ones, the key to inner peace becomes clear: The labors of love inside the home are the means to escape from the ravages of stress — even from the world itself. Home is a haven to look forward to: the place where you can find your center again; the labor of your hands that puts love to work.

Zen is not some kind of excitement, but concentration on our usual everyday routine.

— Shunryu Suzuki,
Zen Mind, Beginner's Mind

Meditation Day by Day

While the goal of meditation is to be able to periodically free the mind of its dependence on the outer world, meditative techniques can be used while performing a number of activities. Choosing one of these, or something else you enjoy doing, can help you develop your facility for meditation:

1. Gardening
2. Bicycling
3. Housework, especially repetitive chores such as vacuuming
4. Arranging flowers
5. Exercising
6. Prepping for a meal
7. Playing in the park with the kids

HIGHER-CONSCIOUSNESS HOUSEWORK

The firefighter in the story above uses kitchen work to guard his center, not as a dreaded chore. For him, it is protection from distraction, cultivation for his avocation as a writer. After all, while you cook, you are not able to clean out the car, vacuum the living room, paint the garage, or mow the lawn. You're protected from having to do other things. Learn to love it, and the kitchen will be your ally. Once you know the secret of mindfulness and how to use meditation to achieve centeredness, you are ready to embrace a whole new way of looking at kitchen work.

Every word we speak, thought we have, and action we take can be thought of as sacred. The activities of work and play, thought and feeling, shouts and whispers operate according to the mechanisms of physical law: For every action, there is an opposite and equal reaction. But action of any kind is also a fulfillment of divine law, a universal law of cause and effect by which every utterance and thought has consequences that never end.

This is how the branch of yoga called "karma yoga" reveals the potential holiness or harm of every action. This is the yoga of cause and effect, the Hindu law of karma first mentioned in the Bhagavad Gita and also expressed by Paul to the Galatians: "Whatsoever a man soweth, that shall he also reap." Karma dictates that everything we do creates an effect that will eventually, if not immediately, descend squarely on our shoulders. While the Hindu believes he cannot escape his karma, Christians, Jews, and Moslems believe that God can mitigate the effects of our actions through grace.

Karma yoga says there is no difference between chopping down a tree and tearing open your morning brioche. The missing tree eliminates the shade, affecting the plants that grew beneath the tree. Even by eating the brioche, the world is changed forever. All thought and speech are actions, even the action of pausing while you think the thought, or giving meaning to spoken words. Karma yoga suggests letting each thought, action, and deed be intentionally holy while practicing detachment from expected rewards. Try to take delight in rewards when they come, but avoid

The apparent simplicity of nature that is revealed to be infinite complication itself requires only earth, sunshine, wind, and water for full existence. A man needs no more to be assured a joyous life. In the morning, he awakens easily to find that he has visitors — a breeze that is the breath of God, sunshine that is the glance of the Mother of Life. He eats naturally — grain, seeds, leaves, roots, grasses in all forms. He adds a few grains of salt — a reminder of his briny origin. This and some clear spring water. Nothing more. How simple and uncomplicated a breakfast table.

— George Ohsawa,
Essential Ohsawa

performing actions with expectation or you may miss out on the fun of being truly free in the sweet, creamy center of your life. This practice will help you find and maintain your centeredness, allowing you to be a component of your sacred kitchen.

So, weed the garden, sweep the walk, mince the onions, and scrub the pots, each for its own reward, for your own delight, and for the benefit of others. For these actions are the same as digging a foundation, mincing circuitry onto silicon wafers, or enhancing any kitchen miracle with a dash of salt and pepper.

Let your thoughts and actions be deliberately holy when you next open a five-pound bag of carrots to peel. It's all right to feel happy about it. It's all right to feel giddy in the midst of waxing the floor. It's exquisite to grin excitedly in the sweet, creamy center of those spaces of peace between distracting thoughts as you pick weeds that will only grow back, or wash dishes that will only get dirty again. Let the sheer energy of your connection to the global kitchen thrill you, and let each motion of your hand commemorate the Creator's love.

Now, you can reexamine your sacred kitchen in a new light, because you have two new tools: an energy-enhanced kitchen space and a proven technique for finding your mental centeredness. The next ingredient for a sacred kitchen is diet, finding the centeredness of the food you prepare.

RECIPES FROM A TINY HERB GARDEN

The following recipes evolved from the profusion of basil and other herbs we harvest every summer from our tiny backyard herb garden. Whether you plant forty acres or just a window box, fresh herbs can generously shower you with fragrant, flavorful dividends. Before you begin to prepare the food, take a moment to get yourself into a meditative state, free from all concerns and worries. Link yourself to the Divine Mother through the global kitchen. Be mindful of every step: scrubbing, cleaning, cutting, mixing, and cooking. Think of every step as a work of love, and you are well on your way to having a sacred kitchen.

PESTO DE RESISTANCE

An abundance of basil means lots of pesto in our sacred kitchen. Here's a good basic pesto recipe. Notice that the cheese has been omitted in favor of white miso. However, you can omit the miso and add a little extra salt and pepper, or some grated Romano or Parmesan cheese, if you prefer. In addition to being a sauce for hot cooked pasta, pesto does wonders for grain and vegetable dishes.

2 $1/2$ cups packed basil leaves (about 1 bunch basil, stemmed)
2 garlic cloves
$1/4$ cup pine nuts
1 tablespoon white miso (optional)
Salt to taste
$1/4$ cup olive oil

In a blender or food processor, process the basil and garlic until finely minced. Add the pine nuts, miso (if using), and salt. Process until well pureed. With the machine running, gradually add the oil to form a paste. If not using immediately, transfer to an airtight container and top with a thin layer of olive oil. Cover and store in refrigerator for up to 2 weeks.

Makes about 1 cup

PESTO, TWO

Why stop with basil? Use your imagination and team favorite herbs with complementary nuts for delightful taste sensations. Use raw spinach, parsley, and walnuts for a regional Italian version, or combine mint, almonds, and lemon juice for a Middle Eastern pesto. If you're fortunate enough to find Thai basil, try the recipe below. Toss this with jasmine rice or rice stick noodles and enjoy the symphony of flavors.

2 $1/2$ cups packed Thai basil leaves (1 bunch Thai
   basil, stemmed)
2 garlic cloves
$1/4$ cup roasted, unsalted peanuts
1 teaspoon salt
$1/4$ teaspoon chili paste
Pinch of sugar
$1/4$ cup toasted sesame oil

In a blender or food processor, process the basil and garlic until finely minced. Add the peanuts, salt, chili paste, and sugar. Process until well pureed. With the machine running, gradually add the sesame oil to form a paste. If not using immediately, transfer to an airtight container and top with a thin layer of sesame oil. Cover and store in refrigerator for up to 2 weeks.

Makes about 1 cup

SUMMER SOLSTICE SALAD
WITH GODDESS GREEN HERB DRESSING

Mix and match ingredients according to preference and availability. The idea here is to have a variety of fresh vegetables that can be esthetically arranged to celebrate summer.

3 cups tender lettuce leaves (butter or green leaf)
2 cups mixed salad greens (arugula, chicory, etc.)
$1/4$ cup shredded carrot

$^1/_2$ cup chopped cucumber
1 cup cooked chickpeas
3 cherry tomatoes, halved
2 tablespoons chopped pecans
1 tablespoon chopped fresh basil
1 tablespoon minced fresh parsley
Edible flowers for as garnish (optional)
Goddess Green Herb Dressing (recipe follows)

Divide the greens among 4 large dinner plates and top with all the remaining ingredients except the dressing in a visually pleasing arrangement. Serve the dressing on the side.

Serves 4

GODDESS GREEN HERB DRESSING

2 scallions, chopped
$^1/_4$ cup chopped fresh parsley
1 garlic clove, chopped
1 teaspoon capers, drained
$^1/_2$ cup soft silken tofu
2 tablespoons fresh lemon juice
2 tablespoons balsamic vinegar
2 teaspoons vegetarian Worcestershire sauce
$^1/_2$ teaspoon sugar or a natural sweetener
$^1/_2$ teaspoon Dijon mustard
1 tablespoon minced fresh basil
$^1/_4$ teaspoon salt
$^1/_4$ cup olive oil
$^1/_8$ teaspoon freshly ground pepper
$^1/_8$ teaspoon Tabasco sauce

In a blender or food processor, process the scallions, parsley, garlic, and capers until finely minced. Add the tofu, lemon juice,

Swiftly arose and spread around me the peace and joy and knowledge that passes all the art and argument of the earth; and I know that the hand of God is the elder hand of my own, and I know that the Spirit of God is the eldest brother of my own. . . .

— Walt Whitman,
Leaves of Grass

vinegar, and Worcestershire and process to mix well. Add all the remaining ingredients and blend well. If not using immediately, transfer to an airtight bowl. Cover and refrigerate for up to 1 week.

Makes about 2 cups

Everywhere, wherever
you may find yourself,
you can set up an altar to
God in your mind by
means of prayer.

—*The Way of a Pilgrim*

Zen Food Blessing

Innumerable labors have brought us this meal.
We should know how it comes to us.
In receiving this offering, we consider
whether our practice and virtue are deserving.
Desiring the natural order of mind, we should
be free from hate, greed, and delusion.
We eat to support life and practice the will
of the Divine.

4

Toward a
Centered Cuisine

*To master the art of cooking — to choose the right kinds of foods,
and to combine them properly — is to master the art of life, for
the greatness and destiny of all people reflects and is limited
by the quality of their daily food.*

— Michio Kushi, in *The Changing Seasons Macrobiotic
Cookbook,* Aveline Kushi and Wendy Esko

I n order to discover the sacredness of the kitchen, we need to crystallize the
concept that the cook is a conduit of chi (the life force) — as dynamic an element in the preparation of a meal as the physical arrangement of the space or
even the food and fire. Becoming as centered as possible is the key to benefiting
from this sacredness: experiencing peace in the very work of the kitchen itself.
But this experience will come more easily with an understanding of the vital role
that food plays in your overall well-being and the abiding spirit of your household. This chapter explores the importance of "centeredness" in what we cook
and how we eat.

A DINNER TO REMEMBER

There is a legend that the Buddha, on his deathbed, could remember only two meals in his life.

During the first twenty-nine years of his life, as the young Prince Siddhartha, the Buddha-to-be had been protected from the world by his father in a magnificent pleasure palace that he never left. Every day the palace was refreshed with fragrant flowers, and even from childhood, Siddhartha was surrounded by more beautiful concubines than he could count. He knew only pleasure throughout his teenage years and twenties. He was cooled when the weather was hot, and warmed when it turned cold. His father had vowed to keep him completely free of discomfort throughout his life. In fact, he swore that Siddhartha would never know anything about the misery of the world outside. In his twenties, Siddhartha married, and his wife bore a son.

Siddhartha began to wonder, however, what life was like beyond the palace walls. He secretly arranged several trips into the outside world, and the misery he saw there inspired him to spend the rest of his life seeking a solution for the suffering of humanity.

Finally, he left the palace dressed in the rags of a beggar, eagerly exploring life without possessions, comforts, food, or sex. So ascetic was he and so passionate in his exploration of suffering that he starved himself nearly to death. But a teenage girl happened by and gave him a dish of rice, which saved his life. This was the first meal the Buddha would remember. After all the sumptuous meals he'd enjoyed in his father's palace, it was as though he had never eaten until that day.

After many years of teaching and traveling, Siddhartha, now the fully enlightened Buddha, found himself in a village called Papa. He'd been invited to eat with a group that had excitedly gathered at the home of Cunda, a smith. Cunda and his wife prepared a meal of rice and mushrooms, but when it came time to eat, the Buddha said to the people that only he would eat. Puzzled, everyone sat quietly as the Buddha taught and ate. But the Buddha fell ill, for, unknown to the smith, the mushrooms were poisonous. The second of the two meals the Buddha could recall on his deathbed was this meal — the one that would kill him.

The Enlightened One had so freed himself from the shackles of worldly desires that he could only remember these two meals. Such detachment is an example of mental "centeredness," a sound guiding principle for anyone who would unite body, mind, and spirit in order to live life more fully, operate with wisdom, and enjoy life in the best of health. From a centered vantage point, it is easier to make judgments, be creative, and know your true place in the world. It is important to realize that nothing throws us off center more than an uncentered diet.

FINDING THE CENTER OF FOOD

A centered person is one whose thoughts are focused, not scattered; someone who resides in a place of peace within, rather than bobbing in the choppy waters of ill health and emotional volatility. Just as a centered individual makes the best friend, student, or parent, such an individual also makes the best cook. We can shift our lives "closer to the center" just by being aware of the great benefits of centeredness. Making the diet more centered is perhaps the greatest consideration in creating a sacred kitchen.

Our greatest challenge as we enter the twenty-first century will be keeping ourselves healthy in an increasingly out-of-balance world. We can see the effects of imbalance in social disorder: Rampant violence, the absence of moderation, and unhealthy competition and acquisition abound in today's society of extremes.

> Cooking is one of those arts which most require to be done by persons of a religious nature.
>
> — Alfred North Whitehead

Food as energy is one way we can think about food. Energy determines the degree and quality of life force that food contains and how much it can give us. Life-giving foods provide us with optimum health by bestowing on us inner healing powers. Keeping the immune system healthy and strong will be a necessity as we enter the twenty-first century.

— Sensei Shigeru Kanai, a Japanese Buddhist priest of the Butsungenshyu sect, *The Path to Self-Healing: Sotaiho*

I once believed that eating healthy meant eating food that was missing something — taste. I once believed eating healthy meant being unsatisfied. I once believed eating healthy meant no security, no comfort, no love.

— Oprah Winfrey

Diet reflects a society. A society reflects its diet.

The solution to these trends is increasingly expressed among spiritual and medical authorities alike. Swami Satchidananda, the founder of Integral Yoga® International, teaches the yogic view on the true function of food: "There are three conditions that food should meet: It should help your mind maintain its tranquillity; it should not stiffen the body with toxins; and it should be able to be digested quickly without wasting a lot of energy." Such food would contain no stimulants, chemicals, artificial hormones, or intoxicants, nor would it contain animal products, as they take a long time to digest and consume a lot of the body's energy to digest. The food would be fresh, organically and locally grown, and comprise primarily whole grains, vegetables, and fruits. This is centered cuisine in a nutshell.

No one is anxious to adopt drastic changes that will alienate friends and family at mealtime, so gentle modifications may be the best plan, unless everyone involved agrees. Whether you make just a few modifications in your diet or plan to make major changes, you'll be happy to know that eating a more centered diet doesn't have to signal the end of fine dining as you know it. The results of this approach can help anyone improve the way they eat. You may even find yourself eating better than you did before.

A centered cuisine must be practical for our time and place, a synthesis of the best examples of healthy diets, from ancient systems to modern medical opinion. Eating centered foods will help you keep physically, mentally, and emotionally centered and remain so, whether you are a homemaker, a business executive, an athlete — or all three. You are, of course, free to accept as much or as little of this dietary wisdom as you wish. The best way to stick to any new regimen, however, is to want to do it. Find the desire within to see what it's like to feel good all over.

"Centered" means balanced, or not to the extreme. Whether we realize it or not, when we eat uncentered foods, it throws our bodies out of balance. The effects may range from simply making us feel "out of sorts" to actually causing physical illness. Sometimes, this uncentered effect can go on for years. In *Creating Health: Beyond Prevention, Toward Perfection,* author and physician

Deepak Chopra, M.D., advises: "People who do not feel sufficient respect for eating are showing no awareness of the flow of organizing power that it represents. Eating indiscriminately or eating unconsciously, eating on the run, habitually overeating or not eating at all — these are all violations of natural law, that is, of the biological processes that must work in their preordained channels in order for food to be converted into us."

Reversing this condition is most successfully accomplished by developing for yourself a centered cuisine that is both healthy and delicious. Since the United States Department of Agriculture (USDA) revealed its radically revised nutritional guidelines in 1992, called the Food Guide Pyramid, even mainstream America has turned its attention toward cleaning up its diet. People have rediscovered certain ancient dietary systems as well and adopted some innovative programs based on them.

Most people find it tough enough to get through the day without having to remember some complicated new thought system or dietary philosophy. But creating a sacred kitchen in your home doesn't require this. It's a simple question of being aware of the ideal goals and, as often as possible, making better food choices. Do this, and degree by degree your life will improve.

Popular diets have come and gone over the years. Many, such as the Pritikin and Atkins diets, were developed primarily for the purpose of weight loss. Others, such as the raw foods regimen, popularized by Ann Wigmore with her Hippocrates Diet and Health Program, may seem more practical to many as a temporary detoxification plan. The Fit for Life diet of Harvey and Marilyn Diamond enjoyed wide notice during the mid-1980s, and various food-combining and body-type diets, such as The Zone and Eat Right 4 Your Type, continue to emerge. This chapter briefly examines a few of the classic lifestyle diets, rather than fad diets or weight-loss diets, although weight loss is often an added benefit from a change to a more healthy lifestyle.

An overview of viable diets, philosophies, and programs can help you gain an intuitive sense of how to make your diet more centered from day to day. We will examine the most strict regimens first and gradually discover how we can custom design a centered cuisine for our personal kitchen.

We will look at macrobiotics, ayurveda, the vegetarian and vegan perspectives, diets developed by Dean Ornish, M.D., and John A. McDougall, M.D. (pioneers in the use of a plant-based diet as a treatment plan to cure disease), and the USDA Food Guide Pyramid to discover what they have in common. The goal is to maximize the beneficial effects of enhancing the life force of the food we eat, and to keep to a minimum the uncentered, unbalanced meals being prepared in our kitchens.

MACROBIOTICS: THE YIN AND YANG OF IT

One of the most ancient diet systems on record was first described in *The Yellow Emperor's Classic of Chinese Medicine*, a seventh-century B.C. text that organized foods by their yin and yang characteristics. It is the primary source of macrobiotics, a lifestyle philosophy developed in Japan by philosopher George Ohsawa and brought to the United States during the 1960s. At that time, a brown rice fast offered by Ohsawa to his toxic American students became a short-lived fad due to some misinformed media attention. Macrobiotics received some unjustified negative publicity, because it was incorrectly reported that this fast was the entire diet. However the diet has since become well known in North America through the work of healers Herman Aihara and Michio Kushi.

Macrobiotics classifies all foods into yin and yang, a principle that actually predates Taoism. The word comes from Greek words

The Taoist Yin-Yang

The ancient Yin-Yang is a symbol for centerdness. Every quality, condition, or substance contains an element of its opposite. When out of balance, any aspect of life, including diet, is incomplete and subject to the effects of extremes.

Figure 4.1

meaning "long life." Also known as the unifying principle of complementing opposites, this concept explains all of nature as having either yin (feminine, recessive, reflective) qualities or yang (masculine, active, aggressive) qualities. In *Whole Food Facts*, author Evelyn Roehl writes, "At the heart of macrobiotic philosophy is the concept of balance. To maintain balance one must choose elements in life that accommodate change. . . . When the forces of yin and yang are balanced, we are healthy."

Yin is cooler, softer, and more passive, while yang is hotter, harder, and more energetic. In foods, the most extreme yin substance is sugar, while the most extreme yang substance is red meat. Even within each category, some items are more yin or yang than others. Among the grains, for example, the most yin is corn and the most yang is buckwheat. Brown rice is the closest to the center. These principles provide a yardstick as we strive to define centered cuisine (see Figure 4.2).

> Let us make our bodies healthy with righteous food. We can thus enter into the miracles of the universe and enjoy a profound eternal life.
>
> — George Ohsawa, *Macrobiotic Guidebook for Living*

The Yin and Yang of Foods Simplified

YIN	CENTERED	YANG
Dairy foods	Whole grains	Meats
Tropical fruits	Beans	Poultry
Tropical nuts	Vegetable	Fish and seafood
Alcohol	Fruits	Eggs
Sugar	Seeds and nuts	

Figure 4.2

This chart is an overview of the yin and yang aspects of main food categories. Foods in the center column are the more centered, according to the macrobiotic philosophy. To keep your diet more centered, eat foods mostly from the center column. This is also consistent with the USDA Food Guide Pyramid.

At its purest, macrobiotics can be a difficult commitment to make. Brown rice is the staple and is usually served with steamed or stir-fried vegetables. Fermented foods are included, such as miso (soybean paste) and tempeh (compressed soybean cakes), and miso soup is often taken at breakfast. Meat is never eaten, but some fish is allowed, as are plant proteins such as tofu, seitan (wheat-meat), and beans. The macrobiotic diet also avoids sugar, dairy, and caffeine. Trained macrobiotic counselors can use their techniques to diagnose and treat illness by adjusting the diet, which has been used successfully in some cases of AIDS and cancer.

When you eat one extreme, the resulting imbalance makes your body crave the opposite extreme in order to right itself. In other words, eating meat and eggs (yang) can make the body crave a sugary confection or pastry (yin), hence the tradition of a sweet dessert after a meal of meat. It has to do with an out-of-balance body struggling for balance. Our behaviors and habits can all be understood from the perspective of their yin or yang nature, and again, the extremes can place us in jeopardy. Constant shifts from one extreme to another can set up conditions ripe for illness, both mental and physical.

Whether you are interested in giving macrobiotics a try or just investigating it for the purposes of fasting or healing particular ailments, you can greatly improve your overall health by remembering a few of the basics (see Figure 4.3).

Daily Macrobiotic Dietary Recommendations

Macrobiotics allows for occasional use of some types of fish, seasonal fruits, nuts, seeds, and other natural snacks.

Guidelines for daily meals include:

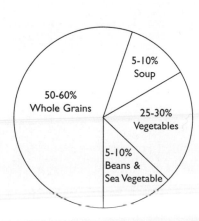

• Whole grains at every meal (try using at least 2 different grains per day)

• 5 to 7 different kinds of vegetables (prepared in various ways: raw, cooked, pickled)

• At least 1 sea vegetable per day (wakame, hijiki, dulse, etc.)

Figure 4.3

• 1 or 2 bowls of soup each day

Simply put, the emphasis of macrobiotics is a truly "balanced" diet that strives to keep our bodies in balance by featuring foods that are more centered in terms of yin and yang, such as whole grains, beans, and vegetables. The theory is that by eating centered foods you can more easily develop balance in every aspect of your life. Eat the extremes, and your life will mirror those extremes in emotional disharmony, aggression, susceptibility to pressure and stress, and the desire for stimulants or depressants. The more centered the foods you eat, the more balanced every aspect of your life will be, from making better business decisions to more effectively managing your relationships.

In addition to yin and yang, macrobiotics classifies foods into five elements: fire, water, wood, metal, and earth. These elements are linked to the seasons, and an understanding of their cycles can help us harmonize with their energies. Various aspects of the macrobiotic diet are shared by the ayurvedic tradition of India, although the two approaches also differ in many ways.

AYURVEDA

The Indian medical and dietary philosophy of ayurveda is another time-honored approach to centeredness. The ayurvedic diet allows a wider variety of foods than macrobiotics. It is a primarily vegetarian approach to eating and healing based on the different human body types. Gaining popularity in the West due to exposure by world-renowned author Dr. Deepak Chopra and others, ayurveda also acknowledges five elements: ether, air, fire, water, and earth. Being Sanskrit-based, it does not use the terms yin and yang, but like Hindu mythology, it recognizes everything in nature as being basically masculine or feminine: *shiva* or *shakti*.

According to ayurveda, the human constitution can be divided into three categories of body type:

Vata: Air and ether. Vata people have quick minds, flexibility, and are creative in their use of resources. They are slight of build, mentally and physically agile, and energetic.

Kapha: Water and earth. These individuals have strong, vibrant

We face serious dangers from our increasingly utilitarian, functional, or "economic" attitudes toward food. True, fast food, TV dinners, and eating on the run save time, meet our needs for "fuel," and provide close to instant gratification. But for these very reasons, they diminish opportunities for conversation, communion, and aesthetic discernment; they thus shortchange the other hungers of the soul. Disposable utensils and paper plates save labor at the price of refinement, and also symbolically deny memory and permanence their rightful places at the table. Meals eaten before the television set turn eating into feeding.

— Leon R. Kass, M.D,
The Hungry Soul

bodies, with the tendency to put on weight. They digest slowly, are tolerant, calm, and loving. They are easy-going but can't be pushed too far.

Pitta: Fire and water. Pitta people are of medium height and slender body and build. They have a strong metabolism and good digestion. They have sharp minds and strong appetites, have high ambitions, and tend to be emotional.

The Principles of Ayurvedic Nutrition

According to ayurvedic tradition, foods need to be:

1. Usually cooked
2. Tasty and easy to digest
3. Eaten in the proper amounts, not too much or too little
4. Eaten on an empty stomach, after your last meal has been digested
5. Eaten in pleasant surroundings with the proper equipment for their enjoyment
6. Complimentary, not contradicting one another in their actions
7. Eaten under relaxed conditions
8. Not eaten during a meal that goes on too long
9. Chosen to nourish your particular constitution and mental and emotional temperament

Every individual is of one type or another or a combination of two. Once a person's type is established, he or she follows a certain dietary guideline for that type, and thereby stays healthy. For example, kapha people should avoid dairy and oil. They should have a light breakfast that includes fruit, and a lunch and dinner of grains, beans, and spicy foods. Pitta people can eat lots of fruits and can have some dairy products. But they should avoid caffeine and fried foods, red meat, and spicy foods. Vata types should minimize their consumption of raw foods and beans and emphasize sweet, sour, and saltiness in foods. Cooked whole grains are especially good for vata types.

This brief overview of some of the basic ayurvedic principles could mislead the reader into believing that ayurveda is easy to learn or adopt, but like macrobiotics, it requires much study to implement correctly. Ayurveda is primarily a medical system designed to keep people healthy and to correct unhealthy conditions that appear in the body. Like macrobiotics, ayurveda emphasizes the consumption of fresh seasonal vegetables, fruits, and whole grains. Its advocates consider it to be a holistic science that takes into account the entire physical, mental, and spiritual aspects of the individual. As with macrobiotics, ayurveda can help healthy people remain healthy and ill people become healed.

VEGETARIANS AND VEGANS

Over the past twenty years, we have seen the vegetarian diet go from fad to mainstream. As more and more people merely cut down on their consumption of red meat and dairy, still others are going "cold turkey" by eliminating most or all animal products from their diet.

Cindy and Pete Kube of Virginia Beach, Virginia, switched to a vegetarian diet in 1992 after their oldest child, Kirsten, then four, started asking questions about where meat comes from. The Kubes are now a healthy vegetarian family, with their youngest daughter, Brooke, having been raised vegan since infancy. Cindy says that six-year-old Brooke has never had ear infections, colic, or most other childhood illnesses. She's so healthy, in fact, that a pediatrician's nurse once remarked, "Are you *sure* you never eat meat?"

Even though much of the world maintains a mostly vegetarian diet, it is only in the past decade that we've seen the number of vegetarians in America skyrocket. According to *Vegetarian Times* magazine (circulation 1 million), as of 1998 there are more than 12.4 million practicing vegetarians in the United States. A recent Gallup poll confirms that each week another thirteen thousand people quit eating red meat. Beef consumption is down 28 percent since 1976. Supermarkets, which even two or three years ago wouldn't carry a block of tofu, now stock a selection of innovative alternatives to meat and dairy. Marketing Intelligence, a

> I do feel that spiritual progress does demand at some stage that we should cease to kill our fellow creatures for the satisfaction of our bodily wants.
>
> — Mahatma Gandhi

The ideal diet is also related to stress in our daily lives, about life and ourselves, and our inner life, or spiritual outlook. Diet, especially vegetarianism, relates to ethics and morals as well. It is therefore not possible to say that the ideal diet always includes a given set of foods or always excludes certain foods. And there is no prescriptive "ideal diet" that is right for everyone, although there are basic principles that apply to the ideal.

— Ron Pickarski,
Friendly Foods

product-reporting firm, predicted that ninety-three new items with either "vegetarian" or "meatless" in their names would debut by the end of 1998 — a 290 percent increase since 1990.

Because a vegetarian diet has been proven to play a role in cardiovascular disease and some cancers, doctors are recommending a shift away from meat and toward a more vegetarian diet. Many stores in larger towns and cities now have fairly complete natural foods sections. In addition, vegetarian entrées are now commonplace on many American restaurant menus, and ethnic cuisines such as Chinese, Thai, and Indian, which include many vegetarian selections, have established themselves in most communities.

Dairy consumption can prevent the absorption of nutrients and are acid-forming in the body. (A balance between acid and alkaline is the ideal for good health.) The pollutants, antibiotics, and bovine growth hormone fed to cattle are passed on to us in meat and dairy products. This results in a decrease in the effectiveness of antibiotics when we need them to treat illness. These hormones are also the cause of sexual maturity in children occurring at earlier and earlier ages. In the 1998 edition of Dr. Benjamin Spock's world-famous baby book, he stated, "I no longer recommend dairy products after the age of two years. Other calcium sources offer many advantages that dairy products do not have." About diet in general, Dr. Spock stated, "We now know that there are harmful effects of a meaty diet. Children can get plenty of protein and iron from vegetables, beans, and other plant foods that avoid the fat and cholesterol that are in animal products."

Generally speaking, a vegetarian is one whose diet consists mainly of foods from the plant kingdom, including vegetables, grains, legumes, fruits, and nuts. Some vegetarians also include dairy products and eggs in their diet, even though they exclude flesh foods.

The following terms are used to differentiate the varieties of vegetarians:

Fruitarian (fructarian): One who eats fruits, nuts, berries, and some vegetables, as long as they are taken from plants that continue to live. Some fruitarians eat only raw foods.

Lacto-vegetarian: One who eats plant foods and dairy products, but no eggs.

Lacto-ovo vegetarian: a vegetarian who also consumes dairy products and eggs.

Vegan: A vegetarian who eats foods only of plant origin. Vegans do not eat dairy products or eggs, or even use products derived from animals (leather goods, fur, or honey).

There are also people who identify themselves as semi-vegetarians (those who are primarily vegetarian but eat meat occasionally) and pesco-vegetarians (people who are primarily vegetarian but include some fish in their diet).

There are as many reasons to be a vegetarian as there are types of vegetarians. One of the most compelling reasons is health. After all, consumption of soy protein in particular has been shown through many scientific studies to reduce cholesterol, relieve symptoms of menopause, and help prevent osteoporosis and heart disease. In Japan, where soy protein has been a dietary mainstay for centuries, there is no word for "hot flash." Statistics show that most Asians live longer than Caucasians and African-Americans, and deaths from heart disease and many forms of cancer have historically been very low. Unfortunately, as the Japanese diet increasingly becomes more westernized, through an increase in meat, poultry, and egg consumption and a decrease in plant-food consumption, health problems from Western diseases increase as well.

The Sherpas, whose rugged endurance on Himalayan mountain expeditions is well known, maintain a diet consisting mainly of grains and lentils in addition to greens, potatoes, and yak's milk. While meat is occasionally eaten, it is avoided completely by the many strict Buddhists among them.

Whether for reasons of health, economics, ethics, or cultural or environmental beliefs, going vegetarian is clearly a personal lifestyle choice. Whatever the reason, the more you lean toward healthful foods, the more centered or balanced, your body will be, which will make it easier for you to achieve centeredness and balance in your mind and emotions.

THE FOOD ITSELF

Now, what about dinner? Is there a type of food or a way of cooking that can enhance our awareness of the life force and the flow of chi through our kitchens?

During the 1980s, our attitudes about food and health underwent dramatic changes, which helped to bring harmony into other areas of our lives as well. Our shift to a vegetarian diet provided countless benefits to our physical health, but also made us feel better about ourselves in other ways. We felt that the change had raised our consciousness about food.

Fodor's travel guides now identify hotels and restaurants that offer vegetarian fare. As vegetarian restaurants and cookbooks become more mainstream, millions of other people are making changes in the way they eat — and the way they think about food, eating, diet, and nutrition.

Every week, it seems, a new study is being reported that contradicts the last one you read, about this food being good and that one being bad. As a result of a rash of poisonings from mass-produced meats and juices, people everywhere are reading labels cautiously in order to defend themselves against self-adapting bacteria such as E. coli and an arsenal of additives. Fast-food chains are test-marketing meat-free burgers and adding pasta dishes to their menus. (We'll look at the role of the sacred kitchen in the environment in chapter 6.)

The picture of our society's health and happiness is clearly on the upswing, but even if you are already serving better food in your home, how often is food chosen for convenience, or for the momentary pleasure it can provide, rather than for its balancing or nutritional effect? How often it is cooked just to be eaten quickly, so you can move on to more important activities?

What can we do in our own lives to offset the following familiar scenes? Hungry teenagers brooding while wolfing down pizza, as the radio blasts; a business luncheon in which stress and pressure create butterflies in already queasy stomachs; a whole family arguing throughout dinner from the first bite of salad to the last bite of dessert; the television set blaring and flashing, with forks and knives on automatic.

We often treat food as incidental in our lives, without a thought to the real value, the miracle, of what it is: living energy from the World Mother without which we could not live.

Depending on where you choose to read about it, it has been known for centuries by some cultures that what we eat and the circumstances surrounding mealtime can have a direct bearing on our mental and physical health. Eating poor food in a disharmonious atmosphere can deteriorate health over time. Likewise, eating centered foods in an atmosphere of harmony can enhance our health, peace of mind, and our longevity, too. A bite of dinner is only a moment on the lips, but its essence is ancient and its effect eternal.

THE MODERN DIETARY SHIFT

How can the body and mind possibly find balance in people who ingest chemical- and hormone-laden flesh products, refined sugars, processed foods, caffeine, and junk food? Perhaps a better question here is: When these substances are replaced by fresh, unprocessed foods in the form of whole grains and seasonal vegetables, can we expect to see more peace and balance in our lives, communities, and society?

Modern medical opinion is coming full circle on this question. It cannot be a coincidence that people are being urged away from meat consumption and toward grain- and vegetable-based diets. Many mainstream medical authorities are even becoming more holistic in their approach to health. In addition to proper nutrition and exercise, many doctors now prescribe using stress management techniques and cultivating a positive attitude in their overall prescriptions for good health. Additionally, medical schools are teaching alternative medicine, while many conventional doctors now offer alternative practices with the traditional.

While ancient dietary and healing systems such as macrobiotics and ayurveda are enjoying renewed interest, a new generation of medical doctors is blazing the trail to health with low-fat and no-fat dietary guidelines.

The work of Dean Ornish, M.D., has had a distinct impact on how diet is used in the treatment of disease. In 1996, he served as a dietary consultant to the White House, and his Program for Reversing Heart Disease prompted forty major insurance companies to cover his program as an alternative to cardiovascular surgery. The program is based on a low-fat vegetarian diet in combination with yoga and meditation.

In his book *Eat More, Weigh Less*, he writes, "Meditation is a powerful tool for increasing awareness. There is an old Zen saying, 'How you do anything is how you do everything.' When you rush through meals, you are likely to rush through life."

Ornish calls his diet the Life Choice Diet, and it is based on *types* of food rather than *amounts*. In addition to being low in fat, the foods contain no cholesterol, consisting mainly of grains, vegetables, and fruits. The diet uses no meat, dairy, or even oils in cooking. It is high in fiber and complex carbohydrates, and in addition to maintaining general good health, it works well for weight loss. In the December 16, 1998, *Journal of the American Medical Association,* Ornish and his colleagues reported that after five years, two-thirds of the original patients stayed with the diet and lifestyle program and their health steadily improved. Patients who had been assigned to conventional care steadily worsened.

Another medical doctor who has helped to popularize a low-fat diet for the prevention and treatment of illness is John McDougall, M.D., creator of The McDougall Program. He, too, was one of the medical pioneers that showed how a low-fat diet can reverse and prevent health problems. The program is similar to Ornish's. The foods are chosen for their innate healing powers. McDougall originally developed the diet to treat a variety of conditions and illness such as osteoporosis, diabetes, high blood pressure, and high cholesterol. The diet is for healing, general health, and illness prevention, and also results in weight loss. The diet was rated as the best overall weight-loss plan by the Physician's Committee for Responsible Medicine (PCRM).

When medical authorities such as Drs. Ornish and McDougall

recommend low-fat or no-fat diets, they are, in fact, recommending a vegetarian diet, one that is free of animal fat and cholesterol. Neal Barnard, M.D., president of the PCRM, also advocates a meatless diet in his book *Food for Life*, in which he writes: "The power foods are foods from plants. Vegetarians have a much better menu for the heart. Lacto-ovo-vegetarians (those who shun meats, poultry, and fish, but consume dairy products and eggs) do much better than those on lean meat diets, while pure vegetarians who steer clear of all animal products do best of all."

For these reasons, all the recipes in this book are made without meat or dairy. There is no loss of flavor or variety, yet there are tremendous gains in keeping the body free of food-caused illness and keeping people more centered. To underscore its importance, we look to John Robbins, who wrote in his book *Diet for a New America*: "We've always known that it was best to eat a 'balanced diet,' but now we are finding out just what a balanced diet really is, and it's not at all what we had thought. Thousands of impeccably conducted modern research studies now reveal that the traditional assumptions regarding our need for meats, dairy products, and eggs have been in error. In fact it is an excess of these very foods, which had once been thought to be the foundations of good eating habits, that is responsible for the epidemics of heart disease, cancer, osteoporosis, and many other diseases of our time."

Essential to any discussion of a modern dietary shift is the quality of the foodstuffs themselves. Nutrition experts agree that whole foods raised organically are the ideal. "Whole foods" are foods found in their whole, natural state, or as close to it as possible, as opposed to a processed, altered, or refined state. They provide optimum nutritional benefit.

Organic refers to the style of farming by which the foods were grown. Organic foods are raised without the use of pesticides, synthetic fertilizers, or other toxic chemicals. They are often thought of as whole foods, but they aren't always the same. A potato, for example, is a whole food, even when grown with chemicals.

Organic foods can be expensive, or even unavailable in your area. This is an aspect of centered cuisine in which you must "do the best you can." Some discrimination must also be used, as processors, manufacturers, distributors, and even some farmers may falsely use the term *organic* on labels for their products.

Proponents of the raw-foods movement maintain that the best nutrition comes from eating foods that have had no cooking whatever. This is based on the belief that the highest possible nutrition and life force is found in fresh, organically grown, raw, or "live," foods, since research has shown that many nutrients are destroyed or diminished by the cooking process.

Clearly, these medically based diet and health programs point to a consensus that a "centered" cuisine is one that relies as much as possible, again, on organically grown whole grains, fresh vegetables, and fruits, and that eliminates consumption of chemical additives, meat, and dairy products.

THE FOOD GUIDE PYRAMID

The push by medical doctors toward a healthier diet for Americans became so intense by 1992, that the federal government, under tremendous pressure from the beef and dairy industries *not* to do so, revised its dietary guidelines away from meat consumption.

The old Food Group Chart, which was dutifully posted in most American classrooms during the post-war years, had little to do with correct nutrition. The chart was actually the result of an advertising scheme devised by the meat and dairy industries in 1956 and sanctioned by the USDA. That chart remained in use until the new Food Guide Pyramid was created (see Figure 4.4), and has now replaced the old Food Group Chart in pediatrician's offices, classrooms, and TV commercials.

The new Food Guide Pyramid is an important step forward toward national guidelines for a more centered diet. In keeping with many healthful dietary philosophies, the pyramid shows the daily servings of food intake, emphasizing grains, vegetables, and fruit. In addition, the U.S. government now recognizes vegetarianism as a "healthy" diet for Americans.

The USDA Food Guide Pyramid

Source: U.S. Department of Agriculture/U.S. Department of Health and Human Services.

Figure 4.4

The old food group chart recommended that 50 percent of the daily intake of food should consist of animal products. In fact, the human body has no nutritional need for animal flesh or cow's milk, which are actually acquired tastes, or learned behavior.

Our very physiology suggests that we are not best suited to eating animal flesh. Humans have the sliding jaw, grinding molars, less-acid stomach, and long intestine of the herbivore, not the vertical hinged jaw, fanged teeth, strong stomach acid, and short intestine of the carnivore. According to Dr. C. Everett Koop, former Surgeon General of the United States, eight of the ten leading causes of disease in 1996 were diet related.

A common myth about meat-eating is that "you need meat to get enough protein." Documented studies show that only about 10 percent of our diet needs to be in the form of protein. Most Americans eat twice as much protein than they need each day. Additionally, we can still get all the protein we need from a grain- and vegetable-based diet. For example, it is now widely recognized that soybeans contain all the essential amino acids of complete proteins.

Did you ever wonder where cows get their protein to grow into such strong muscular animals? They get it from the grains and grasses, just as we can. But those who depend on meat get this vegetable protein secondhand, by eating the flesh of the *animal* who ate the grain and grass. Along with the grain, however, the animal has also been given synthetic hormones, antibiotics, pesticides, fertilizers, and sometimes the ground-up bodies of dead or diseased animals. When we eat animal flesh, therefore, we move far away indeed from the center.

Thanks to television advertising, many people fear that if they don't drink milk, they won't get enough calcium or maintain a youthful appearance. Little do they know that calcium is found in abundance in tofu, nuts, sea vegetables such as kelp and nori, and many land-grown vegetables such as broccoli and dark leafy greens. The protein in milk actually *inhibits* the body's ability to absorb calcium from the milk. Dairy consumption has been linked to heart disease, cancers (especially breast cancer), allergies, sinus trouble, migraine headaches, psoriasis, and much more. Dairy foods cause the body to create an excess of mucus, which can host cold and virus germs in the respiratory tract. Many doctors now question the belief that dairy products are the best way to prevent osteoporosis since it is, in fact, a disease that can be caused by consuming too much animal protein.

You don't have to become a vegan or even a vegetarian in order to maintain a sacred kitchen. But ancient traditions, new medical guidelines, and even the federal government now urge a shift away from heavy meat and dairy consumption. Evidence overwhelmingly suggests that the closer to a vegetarian diet you can achieve, the more centered you will be in terms of physical health. The key is to try to make better choices, every day or every week, to bring your life and health back closer to the center.

Perhaps Cecile Tovah Levin says it best in *Cooking for Regeneration*: "Food is life. Life is food. That which does not sustain life, health, integrity, joy, and peace is not the best food for mankind. Since food creates us, food can also heal us. Right food creates healing and balance; wrong food creates degeneration and decay. Wrong food can destroy us. It can destroy our lives."

Now that we have explored various aspects of ancient and modern centered diets, there is a foundation on which you can develop a centered cuisine for your home. This means a centered diet that has the added appeal of taste and appearance, created with classic cooking techniques.

A CUISINE YOU CAN LIVE WITH

The hardest part of changing one's diet is breaking the old habits. When you've spent a lifetime with a meat and milkshake mind set, you may find yourself rethinking much of what you put into your mouth. Habit, food prejudice, and even addictions all play a part.

As you eliminate the "extreme" foods from your diet, a whole new world of possibilities can open up to you. Once you begin experimenting with new ingredients such as meat and dairy alternatives, you will find it's not necessary to sacrifice the flavor or texture of your favorite dishes. If anything, your retooled recipes can actually taste better because they contain no greasy, hard-to-digest saturated fat.

Whether you're already vegetarian or just want to cut down on red-meat consumption, it is likely that, while you want to improve the quality of your life through what you eat, you also want your food to be satisfying, enjoyable, and simple to prepare.

So, where do you begin? One strategy is to recreate your favorite recipes, but substitute healthier ingredients. Start by making a list of what you usually eat. If you're like many of us, your list may include some family favorites like lasagna, chili, burgers, chicken picatta, fettuccine Alfredo, or cheesecake. No one is going to tell you that a splash of steak sauce on a slab of tofu will taste just like a filet mignon. But it is true that some thinly sliced seitan (wheat meat) sautéed with mushrooms, white wine, and lemon juice, can make a delicious "picatta" entrée. Serve it with a brown rice pilaf and some steamed seasonal vegetables, and you have a centered meal that is stunningly delicious.

We all love a good burger, but most people don't realize they can have a burger made from grains or vegetables instead of ground

Food probably has a very great influence on the condition of men. Wine exercises a more visible influence, food does it more slowly but perhaps just as surely. Who knows if a well-prepared soup was not responsible for the pneumatic pump or a poor one for a war?

— G. C. Lichtenberg, eighteenth-century German physicist and philosopher animal flesh and be just as satisfied. Is it the flesh and grease we love so much, or the bun, onion, tomato, relish, and ketchup? Even fast-food companies sell the "sizzle" and "special sauce," generally playing down the animal their burgers come from.

If you wish to use prepared foods to help with the transition, there are many good products available. A good brand of veggie burgers, when served on a toasted roll with all the trimmings, is just as satisfying in every way as a hamburger. Will you miss your ice cream? Try some tofu- or rice-based frozen dessert and be amazed at the creamy richness. Use silken tofu to make velvety cream sauces and delectable "cheesecakes." Ground-meat alternatives can be used to make chili, tacos, and spaghetti sauce.

A centered diet can begin as simply as swapping some ingredients, and including lots of fresh seasonal vegetables and whole grains along the way. No deprivation, nothing austere. Try some of the recipes in this book to familiarize yourself with ingredients and techniques. Use them as often as you wish — every little bit can help to replace tired old habits with exciting new ones.

With a more centered cuisine, the range of protein sources in your diet can be even more varied than before. Soy foods such as tofu, tempeh, and textured soy protein, along with seitan and the many varieties of beans, are among the protein choices. Grains can include brown rice, basmati rice, millet, quinoa, couscous, barley, and many others.

Exploring ethnic diversity is another great way to achieve variety in your meals along with great taste sensations. Many Mexican, Indonesian, Asian, Indian, and Middle Eastern dishes are or can be adapted to become vegetarian, making use of wonderful combinations of vegetarian ingredients. You can also spice up your life by adding some Indian curry sauce, Jamaican jerk seasoning, or Mexican salsa to an otherwise bland dish. Quick stir-fries, hearty soups and stews, and all manner of salads, sauces, and sautés can be yours for the tasting. Expand your culinary horizons by using healthful and versatile ingredients such as sea vegetables, miso, tahini, buckwheat pasta, and many others. (Refer to the Pantry List for a Centered Cuisine in Appendix I.)

Now for the "cuisine" part. Food prepared in a sacred kitchen can and should aspire to be "haute" in the "highest" sense of the word, whether it be a peanut butter and jelly sandwich or a five-course dinner. This can be accomplished in several ways:

1. Change your attitude while preparing the food (energizing it with love and healing).

2. Use the freshest, best-quality ingredients possible. (The difference between a PBJ made with "balloon bread," generic hydrogenated peanut butter, and a sugary jelly is vastly different from one made from a good-quality whole-grain bread, freshly ground natural peanut butter, and a good-quality fruit-sweetened jam.)

3. Pay special attention to the esthetics of your meal by establishing a sacred ambiance.

SACRED AMBIANCE

Have you ever gone out to dinner and ordered something simple that you could easily make at home, say linguine with marinara sauce? What is it that compels people to go out and spend $11.95 (plus tax and tip) on something they could have made at home for under $2.00? For many, it's the ambiance of the restaurant and the visual appeal of the meal. If your linguine with marinara came served on a chipped mismatched plate, or worse, a pot of pasta slopped with sauce were plunked down on the table, along with a couple of bottles of salad dressing placed on the table for you to glob onto limp lettuce, you'd likely not go back to the restaurant. But isn't that how many of us serve dinner on a busy night when we didn't feel like cooking anyway?

An important element of making centered food into a centered cuisine is to take a few extra moments to add to the ambiance and esthetics of the meal. Start by setting a beautiful table. Go ahead and use the good china; what are you saving it for, anyway? Light some candles and put some fresh flowers on the table, even if just a single stem or a potted plant from elsewhere in the house. Make your table look special and inviting, and everyone will feel special.

Tell me what you eat, and
I will tell you what you
are.

— Brillat-Savarin

Now back to the linguine. That same two dollars worth of pasta can look like a million bucks if you plate it correctly. Take a tip from a chef: Arrange each serving individually; use oversized shallow bowls set on top of large dinner plates. Portion out the pasta and ladle on the sauce smoothly. Garnish with minced fresh herbs and an extra sprig of basil, oregano, or parsley for garnish. Sprinkle some freshly ground pepper around the perimeter of the plate and serve.

The accompanying salad is prepared in much the same way. Serve it first, as in a restaurant — it makes the salad more special and makes dinner last longer for more quality time. Instead of a handful of lettuce in a bowl, arrange the greens on large individual plates. Top with a few colorful garnishes, even if all you have on hand is a carrot to shred and some canned chickpeas. Add a few sunflower seeds for a delightful crunch. Olives, artichoke hearts, or some thawed frozen peas (run them under some hot water for a minute) are also interesting last-minute touches that add nutrition and texture. Have some good homemade salad dressing ready to drizzle on each salad. If you get in the habit of making homemade dressing by the pint or quart, it will always be convenient and you'll eliminate the extra expense of bottled dressings along with their additives.

This is just one way to elevate your home cooking to cuisine. Experiment with unusual ingredients, table service, and garnishes. Add elegant touches, like a basket of fresh hot bread and a dipping bowl of herb-infused olive oil to make a simple meal something special. Place wineglasses filled with spring water and a slice of lemon at each place. Use cloth napkins. Play relaxing music during dinner. Most importantly, whatever you do, do it with love. Your two dollars worth of pasta will suddenly seem priceless.

Overhauling your diet does not have to be traumatic. In fact, it's best to think of it as an adventure. Enjoying a centered cuisine means being free of the ill effects of extreme foods, while striving to meet the challenge to prepare wholesome meals that are interesting, delicious, and even exquisite. This "new" cuisine is as ancient as Creation itself, for: "Behold I have given you every herb-yielding

Turn Your Eating Space into a Centered Dining Experience

Being a "good cook" is only one element to putting a great dinner on the table. There are several other factors that can contribute to a positive dining experience:

1. Ingredients. Use organic, fresh, whole foods with no additives, artificial ingredients, or processing.
2. Attitude. The "secret" ingredient of the best meals is your own loving energy.
3. Variety. Vary cooking methods: sautéing, steaming, baking, broiling, stir-frying, and roasting. Experiment with ethnic dishes, ingredients, and seasonings.
4. Color. Nature's color palette ranges from creamy white mushrooms to deep purple eggplant, and includes vivid oranges, soothing greens, and vibrant reds.
5. Presentation. Learn how to cut vegetables in different ways. Arrange food on plates esthetically. Consult food magazines, cookbooks, and fine restaurants for ideas.
6. Proper tableware. Use a variety of attractive glass and ceramic bowls and plates. Avoid using plastic or metal containers, as they may react with foods.
7. Garnishes. A subtle dusting of spices, a sprinkle of parsley, some minced scallions, or chopped nuts can add color contrast and flavor enhancement.
8. Quality cookware. Stainless steel, cast iron, and earthenware pots and pans are best.
9. Cleanliness. Keep a clean, well-organized kitchen, use well-washed ingredients, and set your table with pride.
10. Table decor. Add a special touch to the ambiance in your dining area with fresh flowers, candles, good table linens.
11. Environment. Remove styrofoam and any toxic materials from your kitchen. Use only filtered or bottled water for washing ingredients and for cooking.
12. Gratitude and good attitude. Express gratitude at meals with a moment of silence, a prayer, or a food blessing. Have pleasant conversations and avoid arguments, worries, and concerns.

seed and every tree, to you it shall be for meat" (Genesis 1:29).

We have explored our own centerdness and that of food, and in the next chapter we will look at the role food plays in sacred celebrations around the world. But first, here are some recipes for a delicious meal featuring tofu, a frequently misunderstood and much maligned source of vegetable protein.

When prepared with love and served beautifully, the following dinner of tofu lasagna will win more accolades than you ever thought possible. No one will miss the meat or cheese, and the health benefits for you and your family will be an added bonus.

Considering we are members of the primate family, most of us eat pretty peculiarly. You won't find gorillas and orangutans tossing unidentifiable animal parts on the grill. They're out in what's left of the rain forests and jungles, eating fresh, organic, locally grown foods that we might only hope to find in health food stores: fruits, vegetables, and nuts that make their hair shine, build phenomenally strong bodies, and help them stay enviably lithe and athletic.

— Ingrid Newkirk,
The Compassionate Cook

Tips for Buying and Storing Fresh Produce

- Grow your own vegetables and harvest them when ripe.
- Grow herbs and sprouts in a window garden.
- Buy organic produce (grown without pesticides).
- Pick your own vegetables and fruits at an organic farm.
- Buy seasonal produce from a farmer's market or roadside stand.
- Buy or pick produce when ripe.
- Judge ripeness by fullness of color, good texture, and correct fragrance.
- Produce should look healthy and unblemished: no bruises, gashes, or moldy spots.
- Leafy greens should be crisp and fresh looking, not wilted or brown.
- Seasonal, locally grown produce (even if nonorganic) is safer than imported.
- Fresh vegetables shipped long distances may actually be less potent than frozen.
- Buy produce that is nonirradiated and without plastic or foam packaging.
- Store ripe produce in the refrigerator; leave unripe produce to ripen at room temperature.
- If using commercial imported produce, discard outer leaves, remove peels, and wash.
- Eat refrigerated fresh foods at room temperature for fuller flavor.

RECIPES FOR CHANGE

If you're ready to make some changes in your diet, but have no idea what to do with tofu, try this simple menu. The main course and dessert look like "the real thing," but contain no cholesterol or saturated fat. The best way to think of tofu is as an ingredient, and not as an end in itself. You wouldn't eat plain flour, but when you combine it with other ingredients, it can become a cake. This is also true of tofu.

Begin with the lovely fresh-tasting salad and move on to the main course: a rich tofu lasagna that will satisfy even a skeptic. The cheesecake is another tofu ambassador. One taste, and people will wonder why they waited so long to try tofu.

FIELD GREENS WITH LEMON-MINT VINAIGRETTE

This salad incorporates a variety of lettuces, herbs, and zesty lemon to create a fresh-tasting salad that is a perfect complement to the lasagna recipe below.

$1/2$ cup olive oil
$1/4$ cup fresh lemon juice
2 tablespoons balsamic vinegar
1 tablespoon minced onion
2 tablespoons minced fresh mint
$1/2$ teaspoon salt or to taste
$1/8$ teaspoon freshly ground white pepper
6 cups mixed salad greens
Sliced cucumber, shredded carrot, and/or black olives
    for garnish

In a small bowl, combine the olive oil, lemon juice, vinegar, onion, mint, salt, and pepper. Whisk together until thoroughly blended and set aside. Portion the greens on serving plates and top with your choice of garnishes, arranged esthetically. Drizzle dressing on top of each salad.

Serves 6

Everyone's Favorite Lasagna

This recipe is a great way to introduce tofu to family and friends. If you like a "meaty" tomato sauce, add some frozen soy "crumbles" (ground beef alternative) or some reconstituted TVP (textured vegetable protein) to your tomato sauce.

1 pound soft tofu, drained and patted dry
1 pound firm tofu, drained and patted dry
$1/4$ cup minced fresh parsley
Salt and freshly ground pepper to taste
3 cups Fresh Tomato Sauce (recipe follows)
$1 1/2$ cups ground beef alternative or TVP (optional)
1 pound lasagna noodles, cooked al dente and drained
1 cup shredded soy mozzarella

Preheat the oven to 350°F. Put the tofu in a large bowl and crumble. Add the parsley, salt, and pepper and mix well. Taste and adjust the seasoning. Spread a layer of tomato sauce in the bottom of a 4-quart rectangular baking dish. Top with a layer of noodles. Top the noodles with a layer of tofu filling. Repeat with another layer of noodles and top with more sauce. Add a layer of ground beef alternative or textured vegetable protein, if using. Repeat the layering process with the remaining filling, noodles, and sauce. Sprinkle the soy mozzarella on top. Bake for 45 minutes, or until bubbly. Remove from the oven and let sit for 5 minutes before cutting.

Serves 8

FRESH TOMATO SAUCE

This sauce is best made with very ripe tomatoes. If you wish, you may peel the tomatoes before chopping. Simply cut an "x" in the bottom of each tomato and plunge the tomato into boiling water for 30 seconds and remove. The skins will come off easily.

1 tablespoon olive oil
1 onion, finely chopped
1 large garlic clove, minced
3 cups chopped ripe tomatoes (about 2 pounds)
One 6-ounce can tomato paste
1 tablespoon chopped fresh basil, or 1 teaspoon dried
    basil
1 teaspoon minced fresh oregano, or $1/4$ teaspoon
    dried oregano
2 cups hot water or vegetable stock
$1/2$ cup dry red wine
1 bay leaf
Salt and freshly ground pepper to taste

Heat the oil in a large saucepan over medium heat. Add the onion and cook, uncovered, until softened, about 5 minutes. Add the garlic and cook 1 minute longer. Stir in the tomatoes, tomato paste, and dried basil and oregano, if using, and cook uncovered for 5 minutes, stirring frequently. Add the water or stock, wine, and bay leaf and bring to a boil, stirring to blend. Reduce heat to low, season with salt and pepper, and simmer uncovered for about 30 minutes, or until the desired consistency is reached. If using fresh basil and oregano, stir in at this time. Taste and adjust the seasoning. Remove the bay leaf before serving. If not using immediately, transfer to a container and allow to cool. Cover and refrigerate for up to 5 days.

Makes about 4 cups

"Say Cheese" Cake

No cheese here — but lots of reasons to smile. For a touch of elegance, serve slices of the cheesecake on a pool of fruit coulis (simply purée some fresh fruit in a blender or food processor), and garnish with fresh berries and a sprig of mint.

For the crust:
1 cup graham cracker crumbs (about 1 crackers)
3 tablespoons soy margarine, melted

For the cake:
3 cups firm silken tofu, patted dry
1 cup sugar or a natural sweetener
$1/4$ cup soy milk
2 tablespoons canola oil
1 tablespoon cornstarch
1 teaspoon vanilla extract
2 cups fruit spread, pie filling, or fruit coulis for topping (see Note)
Mint sprigs and fresh berries for garnish (optional)

To make crust: Preheat the oven to 350°F. Lightly oil a 9-inch springform pan. Place the crumbs in the bottom of the pan, add the melted margarine, and toss with a fork until blended. Press the crumb mixture into the bottom and up the sides of pan. Bake for 5 minutes, or until lightly toasted. Set aside.

In a blender or food processor, process the tofu, sugar or other sweetner, soy milk, oil, cornstarch, and vanilla until smooth. Pour the filling into the prepared crust and bake for 30 minutes, or until firm. Remove from the oven and let cool completely. Spread the desired topping on the cheesecake and refrigerate for at least 2 hours before serving. Serve with topping, over or under each slice, garnished with mint sprigs and berries, if you like.

Food, when seen as medicine for preserving life, has no deleterious side effects. Therefore, if one falls sick, one should first examine one's diet, then choose well, chew carefully, and give thanks. In this way, the curative powers of nature, with which mankind is blessed, are given full reign to act and nearly all diseases are conquered.

— from an ancient book of Chinese medicine, as quoted by Zen Abbess Soei Yoneda in her book *The Heart of Zen Cuisine*

Note: If using fruit spread or pie filling instead of fresh fruit, place it in a small bowl and stir until smooth before spreading it on (or under) the cheesecake.

Serves 8

Bless our hearts
to hear in the breaking of bread
the song of the universe.

— Father John Giuliani, The Benedictine Grange,
West Redding, Connecticut

5

Celebrate!

Any time we eat it's holy.
We should have ritual and ceremony,
not just gobbling down some food to keep alive.

— M. F. K. Fisher

What more do you need in your sacred kitchen besides a higher consciousness of the life force (chi) and keeping your mind and diet more centered? You need celebrations and sacred events to commemorate our holy purpose and keep the kitchen spiritually as well as physically nourishing. The world's sacred traditions warm our hearts and make every meal meaningful and healing in body, mind, and soul. They remind us that, as different as we appear to be, we are really very much alike. In their richness and diversity, we can find common themes by which to personalize the sacred kitchen and honor the Creator in each other — whenever we make something to eat.

Prayer is an intimate
friendship, a frequent
conversation held alone
with the Beloved.

— Saint Teresa of Avila

A MELTING POT TABLEAU

Let's bring the principles of the sacred kitchen down to earth and make them tangible in our homes. To do this, we need to establish a sense of time and place, a form and structure in which to apply them. Fortunately, people of faith the world over offer a rich variety of customs that we can either adopt or adapt.

Whatever our religious background, our traditions keep the cherished values alive by which our ancestors struggled and survived, raised their families, and put food on the table.

As chef/author Ron Pickarski states in his book *Eco-Cuisine*, "Every major religion centers part of its ritual around the meal. With Catholicism, it is the Eucharist; in Judaism, there is the Seder meal; and in India, it is the Bandar. From the onset of civilization humanity has seen food as a gift from its creator (God) and Mother Earth. That is why we begin our meals with a prayer of thanks."

Traditions define our identities as world citizens and connect us to our divine origin and thereby to each other. Traditions, rituals, and customs are the bonds that give sanity and sanctity to our sometimes synthetic lives. They also show how cooking and eating are inexorably tied to everything we do, for in them lies unity, one of the great secrets of human health and happiness. A perfect example of this tie can be found in Robin's northeastern Pennsylvania childhood.

The ethnic diversity of Chicago is well known. It is a city of many nations, whose neighborhoods still recall the rich traditions of the Irish, Polish, Hungarian, Slovak, Lithuanian, Italian, and German immigrants who settled there over a century ago. Each neighborhood has its well-known boundaries, rules, and politics; its restaurants, churches, and taverns. You can get corned beef and cabbage in an Irish pub, *holupki* and *pierogi* in a Polish diner.

Hazleton, Pennsylvania, a small city perched on a mountain ridge, is like Chicago in many ways. The European nations are also represented there: The Irish settled on the south side, the Italians on the north. The Poles, Hungarians, Lithuanians, and Slovaks spread out to the west. Each group has its own churches, grocery stores, schools, and taverns.

The people of Hazleton are descended from hearty immigrants who had been specifically lured there during the mid-1800s to work in the anthracite coal mines. They had come looking for a better life in America, but found instead a form of slavery, working for company scrip with store accounts they could never pay off.

The small city is still rich with the deep religious traditions of the miners who each day never knew if they would come home from work. To them, prayer and gratitude were essential ingredients of every meal, which was served in a kitchen in which not even a scrap was wasted.

Robin grew up in Hazleton's north side, the daughter of an Italian father and a Hungarian mother. Her grandfather had been a respected plastering contractor in the area, and her father became a real-estate developer. Both of her parents were second-generation Europeans. Robin's grandmothers spoke barely a word of English their entire lives.

Her sister Carole married Jim Lazur, the son of a Slovak contract miner, Ed, who was a miner while Jim was growing up. Jim's mother was also Slovak, the daughter of a miner who was instrumental in bringing the International Mine Worker's Union to the area. Robin's extended family still encompasses scores of people throughout the region who practiced a variety of Roman Catholic customs. A rich tableau of those customs came together every year at the Lazur's house, when Robin's extended family celebrated a Christmas Eve Holy Supper.

Family members would work together on the huge meal so no one person would have too much to do. By late afternoon, the pots and casseroles would begin to stream into Carole's kitchen, where they would be kept warm before being brought to the large table set for as many as twenty.

Even before anyone was seated, the table looked full. A holiday centerpiece of fragrant greenery was surrounded by several red candles waiting to be lit. Place settings of the best china and silver were displayed. Also on the table was a small bowl of honey beside a neat stack of unleavened wafers, acquired that afternoon from St. Joseph's, one of the Slovak churches, and blessed by the priest. Still used in the area, the rectangular wafers are about the size of a folded napkin, come in pastel colors, and are embossed with religious scenes. They are made from the same waferlike bread as Roman Catholic communion hosts.

Once everyone was seated, a blessing was read, followed by a quote from the Bible and a handwritten benediction ("good speech"). Then, each one attending, even the children, added to the blessing by turn, praying for families, friends, and for peace in the world. In this Christmas Eve celebration, Jesus Christ was invited to be present and bless the meal. The holy wafers were then passed around the table, and each one dipped his or her wafer into the bowl of honey before passing it.

An extra place setting was always present. The tradition of the empty place was a reminder of Saint Paul's advice to entertain strangers who may be "angels unawares." The empty place also reminded them of loved ones who could not be present, and of a time, during the Great Depression, when a hungry tramp down on his luck would be invited in to join the family for dinner.

The gathering began with some delightful appetizers from the Italian side: hot cherry peppers and mushroom caps stuffed with a spicy bread crumb mixture. The first course consisted of two Slovak soups that are only eaten during Holy Supper: the first, a clear sour mushroom soup and the other, a thick, garlicky white bean soup. Then the main courses followed: From the Italian side came pasta with a rich tomato sauce laden with chunks of *bacala* (codfish) and sprinkled with a special walnut-raisin-bread crumb mixture. Also from the Italian tradition came a plate of batter-dipped fried smelts.

Many of the Hungarian, Polish, and Slovak traditions are similar, so distinctions blurred. Pierogis, those delicate doughy envelopes filled with potato and cheese, prune, or sauerkraut and onion, were sautéed in onions and butter. Also present was a serving bowl heaped with *bobalki*, little dough balls tossed with a sweet mixture of poppy seeds, sugar, honey, and milk. A vegetable dish was usually served, sometimes green beans and other times a salad.

Just when everyone was too full to take another bite, the table was cleared and desserts were brought in. The women who made them carefully unwrapped the trays and placed them in front of the guests. Poppy seed and nut bread, golden sweet pineapple squares, colorfully frosted *viscuit* cookies sprinkled with coconut, tender butter balls made with ground walnuts, and the sublime *kiffels*, tiny Hungarian rolled pastries filled with a sugary nut mixture. There were also delicate Italian crystals — wafer-thin deep-fried dough dusted with powdered sugar — anisette cookies, a tray of red and green Christmas cookies, and some chocolate brownies.

The cherished traditions in Robin's family continue today, even though many parents and grandparents have passed on. But without those living links to the European old world, memories have begun to fade, especially among the new generations. And this seems to be the trend wherever one goes in America. Family traditions are disappearing, one by one. The loss isn't just of the unique foods, but of the holy purpose of the gatherings and the genuine love that was shared.

You can enhance the influence of the sacred kitchen in your home — the life force in the food, your alchemy of attitude, and your centered cuisine — by bringing a sense of sacredness to the table when it's time to eat. If you have no old-world customs in your household, you can borrow from any of the following traditions and adopt those that have meaning for you. The idea is to add a bit of holiness to the everyday and make certain days of the year special with meaningful celebrations that you and your household can create together.

Let's look at some of the world's most cherished customs and discover ways to take them home with us.

THE PEOPLE OF THE BOOK

People throughout the world celebrate the significant events of their lives with food. Some kind of snack is served whenever there is a birth, a death, a coming of age, a birthday, a marriage, a retirement, a graduation, a first hunt, a girl having her ears pierced, or the winning of some prize. We either fire up the village fire pit or the gas grill, bake a cake, or order a cold-cut tray from the deli. Is the human race prompted by its DNA to ritualize even the most trivial of events, or do we just love an excuse to eat?

> Self-restraint and self-command, consideration for others, politeness, fairness, generosity, tact, discernment, good taste, and the art of friendly conversation — all learnable and practiced at the table — enrich and ennoble all of human life.
>
> — Leon R. Kass, M.D,
> *The Hungry Soul*

Be not forgetful to entertain strangers: for thereby some have entertained angels unawares.

— Hebrews 13:2

Many of our rituals, especially in the West, are strictly secular. Even though "Super Bowl Sunday and pizza" would sound impressive in Sanskrit, this ritual only edges into the sacred as fans pray for their favorite teams. But there are other rituals and celebrations that can bring the sacred kitchen to life, and these are deeply rooted in our inescapable connection to our Creator.

For example, celebrations involving food reach back into the very history of the People of the Book: the Jews, the Christians, and the Moslems, whose Holy Scriptures hold the Pentateuch, the first five books of the Bible, in common and hail Abraham as their ancestral patriarch. The peoples who would eventually become the Jews and Christians descended from Isaac, Abraham's son by his wife Sarah; those who would become the Moslems descended from Abraham's son Ishmael by Sarah's handmaid Hagar.

To the devout of the world's major religions, every part of life is revered as a manifestation of the Creator, and this is nowhere more apparent than among the Moslems. Food and eating number among the great blessings of Allah ("God," in Arabic), and this sublime belief is kept in mind whenever a meal is consumed.

Moslems fast during the entire Islamic month of Ramadan, the ninth month of the lunar calendar, and the first month, it is believed, that Mohammed began to receive the Qur'an from Archangel Gabriel. During Ramadan, observant Moslems take no food, drink, tobacco, or sensual pleasure before sundown or after sunrise.

Fasting in Islam was modeled after Jewish fasting until A.D. 624, two years after Mohammed's move from Mecca to Medina, when by Qur'anic revelation he cut off relations with the Medinan

The Five Pillars of Islam

1. Shahada: profession of faith: "There is no god but God, and Mohammed is the Messenger of God."
2. Salat: ritual prayer
3. Zakat: almsgiving
4. Sawm: fasting during the ninth lunar month
5. Hajj: pilgrimage to Mecca

Jews and changed many customs. Ever since, Moslems fast during the day, and Jews fast in the evening.

The obligation of fasting during Ramadan is called *Sawm*, one of the Five Pillars of Islam, and it is a time of abstention, spiritual discipline, self-examination, and forgiveness, analogous in theme to the Jewish High Holy Day of Yom Kippur. When fasting during Ramadan includes abstinence from pleasures other than food, it is believed that devotion is enhanced.

The first new moon after Ramadan signals the end of the Sawm, and the *Eid al-Fitr* begins, which is the festival of "breaking the fast." The festival lasts several days and is marked by feasting, the exchange of gifts, and, of course, plenty of food. During Eid al-Fitr, many traditional foods are served, especially *harira*, a soup of lentils, rice, and chickpeas; yogurt soup; and a sweet vermicelli pudding called *shir khurma*. As always, a grace blessing is spoken at mealtime:

> *All praise to Allah.*
> *Praise to Allah who has filled us,*
> *Quenched our thirst, and*
> *Made us His obedient servants.*

The Jews, perhaps more than any people in the world, observe a host of laws and customs originating in the Torah (Old Testament) that pertains to food, fasting, and prayer. Their talmudic literature (commentaries on observing the Torah) forbids taking nourishment without first offering a blessing, because to do so would constitute stealing from the bounty of the Lord. For thousands of years, Jews have celebrated Passover with a *seder* (SAY-der), a celebration that features a lengthy, elaborate meal (see description later in this chapter).

Observant Jews recite blessings before, during, and after meals. A traditional blessing, *ha-motzi*, is spoken to bless bread (see text on page 42), which honors the memory of manna, the heavenly bread mysteriously provided by God nightly to the Israelites as they wandered in the desert.

It is astonishing to realize how many of Jesus' major miracles

The Story of Manna

The word derives from the ancient Hebrew *man'hu*, which means "What is it?" It is the mysterious food that God provided to the Israelites as they traveled from Egypt to the land of Canaan. The manna rained down from the heavens for six days every week. Every morning, a "fine flake" could be gathered up from the ground, to be consumed only one portion at a time. Exodus 16:31 describes manna as white, similar to coriander seed, and tasting like "wafer and honey." Numbers 11:7 says it was like "gum resin." The manna was ground, boiled, and made into cakes.

involved food and blessings. The Last Supper celebrated by Jesus and the apostles was actually a Passover seder. While Protestants periodically commemorate the Last Supper with communion, Roman Catholicism holds that, as consecrated by the priest during Mass, the bread and wine are mystically transformed into the body and blood of Christ. These are consumed during the ritual sacrament of Holy Eucharist, again, derived from the seder.

Jesus performed his first miracle at the wedding at Cana by turning water into wine. At Bethany, Jesus taught Lazarus' sister Mary while sister Martha complained about having to make dinner by herself. Jesus fed five thousand people in the desert and then four thousand in Galilee by multiplying a handful of loaves and fishes. In each case, Jesus looked up to heaven, blessed the bread with ha-motzi, and gave thanks. The miracle of the multiplication of grain is also ascribed to Elisha in II Kings 4:42–44.

Elisha's Miracle

And there came a man from Baal-shalisha, and brought the man of God bread of the first fruits, twenty loaves of barley, and full ears of corn in the husk thereof. And he said, Give unto the people, that they may eat. And his servitor said, What, should I set this before an hundred men? He said again, Give the people, that they may eat: for thus saith the LORD, They shall eat, and shall leave [thereof]. So he set [it] before them, and they did eat, and left [thereof], according to the word of the LORD.

— II Kings 4:42–44

A PASTICHE OF SACRED TRADITIONS

Whether we live in mainstream or nontraditional households, whether we're working parents or currently without a partner, we all need sacred experiences in our lives to keep us attached to a power greater than ourselves and to keep us coming back to centeredness every day. The best way to open our lives to the sacred is to open our understanding of the ties of sacredness among the world's religious traditions.

As the Hassidim are the mystics of Judaism, the Sufis are the mystics of Islam. In his book *Philosophy, Psychology, Mysticism, and Aphorisms*, the founder of the modern Sufi movement, Hazrat Inayat Khan, wrote, "Instead of doing as the theologians in colleges who only want to find what is the difference between Moses and Buddha, one should look behind all religions to see where they unite, to find out how the followers of all the different religions can be friends, how they can come to that one truth."

With Khan's benevolent spirit in mind, there are certain customs whose elements are especially well suited for use in the sacred kitchen and are easy to adopt or adapt. Let's take a brief world tour and visit some perhaps less well-known ways in which people celebrate Spirit with food.

First, Clean House

Chinese people celebrate the New Year (Spring Festival) shortly after the winter solstice (January–February). The ancient custom seems to unite heaven and earth, because the people worship the Buddha at the same time as they are planting the spring rice.

Our friend Huizhen Zhang is a traveling writer, translator, and teacher who was born in Shanghai and grew up with the traditions of the week-long celebration. While showing us how to make steamed vegetable dumplings during the summer of 1998, she explained that in China, families prepare for New Year's Eve two days before by first thoroughly cleaning the house inside and out. Some families begin even earlier. Then, they make the foods that will be used in their ancient ritual. The cleaning of the house is the clearing of the mind and heart for the purpose of welcoming in the new

> The pious Jew never places food in his mouth without reciting the appropriate benediction, and there are special blessings for bread, for fruit, for vegetables, for cakes and cookies, for wine, and even for water.
>
> — Ben M. Edidin,
> *Jewish Customs and Ceremonies*

O ye who believe! Eat of the good things with which we have supplied you, and give God thanks if ye are His worshippers.

— The Holy Qu'ran, 5:1:2

year and not carrying forward negativity from the previous year.

The older people begin their day with prayer, perhaps visiting the temple with a food offering to Buddha, a habit that is on the wane among young Chinese. Religious faith is stronger in rural areas, she said, as she recalled how her grandparents in the Zhe Jiang Province, one of the richest in China, made their own bean curd by hand with a mill and cooked on a medieval stove. The farm is now run by her aunt and uncle, and large mills can still be seen there being powered by donkeys.

As a child growing up in the city of Shanghai, Huizhen recalls the New Year's Eve preparations that began early in the morning by grinding rice in a small stone mill with her mother and sisters. The process took five hours to create "sticky rice," which was then hung in a cloth bag and squeezed dry. The sticky rice was then used to make foods for the New Year's feast: cookies with sesame seeds, rice balls, or rice in a bowl with fancy vegetables and dried mushrooms. They also made rice dishes with fish, shrimp, and chicken.

Once the dishes were ready, they were placed on the altar that bears a statue or picture of Buddha. Fruits were also placed there, along with spoons and chopsticks for Buddha to use. But before anyone could eat, each family member would pray and individually ask for blessings throughout the year. This occurred around sundown, after an exciting week of preparations.

During Chinese New Year, adults prayed for success and good luck for the new year, and children might pray to do well in school. The food presented to Buddha was considered sacred, and only after worship was complete did the family partake of the savory dishes that took so long to make.

It was the tradition that, during those long hours of preparation, family members spend quality time talking, laughing, and praying together. On New Year's Day, new clothes were worn to begin the new year. In the days that followed, rice fields were prepared for the summer harvest, and the cycles of life and death continued as they have for thousands of years.

Huizhen said that according to the Chinese calendar, the year 1999 is the Year of the Rabbit, and 2000 will be the Year of the Dragon, an auspicious year for China and for the entire world.

To Sweden, from Sicily

Celebrating the Feast of Saint Lucia has been a custom in Sweden for centuries, which is odd, since Lucia herself was Sicilian. She lived around the beginning of Constantine's rule, A.D. 304, and was canonized for her martyrdom. She so loved God that she refused to compromise her chastity. She fastened candles around her head so both hands would be free to carry food to Christians hiding in the caves. Her name means "light," and Saint Lucia is now known as the Queen of Light.

According to legend, she had given all her money to the poor and so was without a dowry. A frustrated suitor had a judge commit her to a brothel. When the soldiers tried to take her away, she was immovable, as though rooted to the spot. The judge then ordered that she be burned on the spot for her steadfast beliefs, but the fire would not light. Finally, she was put to the sword.

In Swedish homes, the Christmas celebration begins on December 13, Saint Lucia's Day. The family elects one of the daughters to be Saint Lucia, who, early that morning, dons a long dress or robe and a crown made of greens and flowers that holds seven lit candles. "Saint Lucia" then leads the other children to the parents' room, singing traditional songs and carrying a tray of coffee and sweet buns that have been specially prepared for the occasion. The buns are made in a variety of shapes and decorated with raisins, fruit, candy, and currants.

A Verse from Saint Lucia's Song

The night is great and silent.
Now hear the sound
In all the quiet rooms,
A rustle as of wings.
See, on the threshold
She stands clad in white
With lights in her hair,
Saint Lucia, Saint Lucia.

Buenos Aires

In parts of the Christian world, Christmas Eve can be more important than Christmas Day. This is true in Buenos Aires, where

Gratitude is heaven itself.

— William Blake

As in the great religions of the East, the Native American makes small distinction between religious activity and the acts of everyday life. The religious ceremony is life itself.

— Peter Matthiessen,
Indian Country

friend Patricia Gershanik grew up. She is a health care professional in Virginia Beach, Virginia, and remembered celebrating Christmas as a child.

In Buenos Aires, families exchange gifts on Christmas Eve, when, at midnight, they cheer before opening them. Traditional foods are eaten such as nuts, a fruitcake-like sweet bread called *pan dulce*, and dried fruits. Some typical drinks for this night are champagne, wines, and *clerico*, a special mixture of fruit with wine or champagne, which is served like punch.

The three kings were the wise men who traveled from afar to bring gifts to the newborn Jesus in Bethlehem. On the evening of Los Reyes Magos, children leave wine for the kings who are expected to visit. They leave water and also some grass for their camels. They put a pair of shoes in a visible place, in which the "kings" leave gifts for the children to discover in the morning.

Though not a sacred fete, Argentineans also celebrate Students' Day on their first day of spring, September 21. On this day, students and teachers fill the parks of the city, have picnics, and celebrate together. It is a day of fun and mutual respect that could uplift the relationships among teachers, students, and the PTA throughout North America.

The Way of Tea

Worlds away from the American coffee break is the tea drinking ceremony of Japan. The Zen tea ceremony was established as an art form in the sixteenth century by Sen Rikyu, considered the greatest of all tea masters. It is an elaborate, sacred experience for those who practice it, based on the adoration of beauty in the daily routine of life, and is an esthetic way of entertaining guests according to a set ritual.

A classic tea ceremony takes place in a tearoom, or *sukiya*, which is often built right into a Japanese home, the earliest versions having been separate structures adjacent to the house. It is simple in design and used specifically for the tea ritual. The room consists of the main tea room, which is generally about nine feet square. There is an anteroom called the *midsuya* where the utensils are washed and arranged before the ceremony, and a portico, or *machiai*, where the guests wait prior to the ceremony.

The ceremony is conducted by a tea master who practices the Zen of estheticism. The rituals of making, pouring, and drinking the tea represent various aspects of Zen doctrines. Lacquered trays, a wooden dipper and linen cloth, a simple flower arrangement that reflects the season of the year, glazed ceramic cups, and a kettle over a brazier are all important elements.

The tea room is a literal example of a ritualized sacred kitchen in which friends gather in an isolated space to drink tea and discuss art, calligraphy, the flower arrangement, and the respected ceremonial implements themselves.

> ## Four Qualities of the Tea Ceremony
>
> Sen Rikyu, who formalized the Zen tea ceremony into an art form in the sixteenth century, emphasized that a tea ceremony should reflect four qualities:
>
> 1. Harmony among the guests and the utensils
> 2. Mutual respect
> 3. Cleanliness, in which guests wash their hands and rinse their mouths
> 4. Tranquility, which includes careful use of each implement

Kwanzaa

Kwanzaa is Swahili for "first fruits of the harvest," and is an African-American cultural celebration created in 1966 to celebrate the culture and customs of those of African heritage. Kwanzaa is celebrated from December 26 through New Year's Day.

Karamu is the name of the lavish feast of Kwanzaa, and it draws on the cuisines of Africa, the Caribbean, and the American South. Dishes are largely made of millet and other grains, yams, peanuts, rice, vegetables, and fruits. In addition to food, the karamu is alive with music and dance, readings, cultural remembrances, and blessings.

One of seven principles is celebrated on each day of Kwanzaa to remind participants of the importance of keeping them active in their lives throughout the year. *Umoja* is unity, and stresses the idea that in racial unity pride and identity can be maintained. *Kujichagulia* is the essential principle of self-determination. Individuals are reminded that they have the power to accomplish their goals, whatever they may be, and do not have to rely on other groups or institutions. *Ujima* is collective responsibility: The group is responsible for what individual members do, and shares in the accomplishments of individuals. *Ujamma* is cooperative economics, wherein community members support the businesses in their community whenever possible, and thereby support each other economically. The principle of *Nia* reinforces the need for purpose in life and in activities. *Kuumba* adds the element of creativity to nourish the soul, and *Imani* is the vital foundation of faith.

In the Kwanzaa celebration, various rituals are performed to formalize participants' dedication to these principles. Here are some of the items used in these ritual celebrations:

- **Kikombe cha umoja:** a communal cup for the libation
- **Kinara:** a seven-branched candleholder symbolizing Africa and its peoples
- **Mishumaa saba:** seven candles symbolizing the principles that African Americans should live by
- **Mazao:** fruits and vegetables to represent the product of the unified effort
- **Mkeka:** a straw place mat, symbolizing the reverence for tradition
- **Vibunzi:** an ear of corn for each child in the family
- **Zawadi:** simple gifts, preferably Africa-influenced, such as a dashiki, a brightly colored tunic

On the African continent itself, holiday feasts vary according to the type of celebration, religious dietary restrictions, and available ingredients. Africans celebrate a variety of communal festivals linked to agricultural milestones. Many African rituals include the worship of ancestors through gods and spirits, and include costumes, dances, and drumming in ritual storytelling perfor-mances. Over the centuries, African Christians and Moslems have combined some of their beliefs with ancestral and tribal modes of worship.

A Day for Saint David

Too few countries in the world have chosen a vegetable to be their national symbol, but Wales chose the leek. The stately member of the onion family is associated with the vegetarian Saint David, who helped the Welshmen defeat the Saxons in the sixth century by telling the soldiers to wear leeks in their hats so they could recognize each other during battle. The Welsh celebrate Saint David's Day on March 1 every year by wearing leeks around their necks or on their hats. They eat pies and soups made with leeks on Saint David's Day.

Saint David spent many years in prayer, practiced asceticism, and preached a message similar to the Hindu idea of karma yoga: There is great holiness in ordinary tasks when the tasks are performed with a conscious, loving intent and compassion, for the greater good of all.

Ahimsa

As you become more centered, you may find you are growing more sensitive to the world around you. Many people who change their diet gradually discover a new reverence for life that they never felt before. This is the essence of *ahimsa*. A concept derived from a Sanskrit word that means "harmlessness to all life," ahimsa means "noninjury" and "the absence of the desire to kill." It is a conscious abstinence from harming or wishing to harm any being. Ahimsa is the bedrock of traditional Indian ethics and is considered to be the highest dharma. Ahimsa was one of the principles that guided the life and accomplishments of Mahatma Gandhi.

The Buddhist world honors compassion in a number of celebrations. Depending on whether the Buddhist, Chinese, Gregorian, or Hindu calendar is being observed, similar customs occur on different dates.

All Soul's Day, on the fifteenth day of the seventh month of the

When I was a boy my parents, grandparents, aunts and uncles would tell me of life.... [I learned that] there are offerings needed along the way. There are songs and prayers needed to help me along, so they taught me some songs and I learned prayers. I learned of sacred places where I go to and make my offerings and give my thanks. Up to this day it has helped me this far. I still am living that life.

— Big Mountain, Navajo elder

Buddhist lunar calendar, is one of the most popular Buddhist festivals. On what is also called the Festival of Ghosts, the faithful join the monks in rescuing suffering souls: those who have passed on and are trapped in the afterlife by their experiences or karma before they died. Christians pray for the dead on All Souls' Day, November 1; however, the Buddhists extend the circle of compassion to animals. Several sects eat vegetarian dishes and refrain from killing and eating animals. They do this on the Buddha's birthday in April also, the same day on which the Hindu Prince Siddhartha attained enlightenment, or Buddhahood.

Thailand, Burma (Myanmar), and Sri Lanka are predominantly Buddhist. They practice a custom called *fang sheng* during Buddhist New Year (March-April). Fang sheng means to "purchase animals and free them." Many Buddhist monasteries have fish ponds for people to bring fish they would set free. In Burma, Buddhists set pet fish and birds free at this time.

Songkran is the Buddhist New Year, or Water Festival, in Thailand. Celebrated when the Sun enters Aries in late March, on this day believers wash away misdeeds with water, literally spraying water on each other in the streets and homes to start clean for the new year. The children show their respect for their elders by sprinkling perfumed water into their hands. Again, pet fish and birds are set free as a symbol of kindness to all living beings.

"Why Is This Night Different?"

Unmatched for its beauty as well as intricacy is the Jewish observance of Passover (Pesach). For thousands of years, the Passover holiday has commemorated the pharaoh's releasing of the Israelites from bondage in Egypt. Passover generally lasts for seven days, depending on how a family or community counts the days, and is a holiday of liberation and hope that brightens Jewish homes every spring.

Passover is the Holiday of Unleavened Bread (matzoh), because when God ordered the Israelites to leave Egypt, there was no time for the dough to rise. They carried matzoh with them as their only food.

Passover consists of three basic rituals that are performed during the seder, a Hebrew word that means "order":

1. Telling the exodus story (the Maggid)
2. Eating matzoh ("At evening you shall eat unleavened bread." Exodus 12:18)
3. Refraining from eating or owning *hametz*, or leavened bread

The seder meal is celebrated on the first night of Passover, and it includes other rituals as well. Bitter herbs are eaten to remind Jews of the bitterness of slavery; drinking four cups of wine or grape juice reminds them of the joy of liberation; and eating the large seder meal is a celebration of the plenty and abundance attributed to God's intervention with the pharaoh.

The liturgy used during the seder is called the Haggadah, and it includes songs, blessings, the reading of the Maggid, and descriptions of the customs the family will use during the celebration. By way of the seder, the story of Passover is passed on from each generation to the next. Part of the great beauty of it is that it involves every member of the household and guests. The Haggadah, for example, gives Four Questions that are to be asked by children who personify various qualities (wise, wicked, simple, and inexperienced), who thereby participate in the successive steps of the seder. Perhaps the best question of all, asked by the father of the children, is: "Why is this night different from all others?" The children answer one by one, and the theme of Passover is emphasized. (It is also said that the children are less likely to fall asleep when they participate!)

Either a single seder plate *(k'arah)* or a separate one for each person, is set at the table, and symbolic foods are placed on it. Any dish can be used, but many families have specially marked ceremonial plates. They are:

1. Karpas: A green vegetable, usually parsley, symbolizing spring and rebirth. It is dipped in saltwater near the beginning of the seder to symbolize the tears of the Israelites in captivity.

2. Maror: Bitter herbs. Horseradish is mixed with endive, romaine, or escarole as a symbol of the bitterness of captivity.

3. Haroset: A mixture of chopped apples, nuts, wine, and spices. The bitter herbs *(maror)* are dipped in the haroset to improve their taste. The haroset symbolizes the mortar that the Israelite slaves used to make bricks in Egypt. Recipes vary around the world.

4. Beitzah: A roasted egg, the symbol of a festival sacrifice offered by Jews going to temple in Jerusalem. (Vegans can use a plastic egg.)

5. Zeroa: A roasted shank bone to symbolize the Passover sacrifice. (The Talmud says that vegetarians can use a broiled beet.)

The cups of wine symbolize expressions of redemption in Exodus. But during the seder, a large, ornate goblet is set aside for Elijah, since according to legend, he visits everyone on Passover and drinks from his cup. Other customs of the seder include periods of reclining, to symbolize the freedom Jews received from the Passover; recitations before, during, and after the festive seder meal; and the ritual "stealing" of some matzoh by a child who is selected to do so. Next to the seder plate, three matzoh crackers are placed. The middle one is broken in two, and the larger piece is wrapped in a napkin and set aside. Now, the child "hides" it, and at the end of the seder the family searches for it.

The matzoh to be hidden symbolizes the "bread of affliction." Breaking it in half represents the poverty of the lives of the Israelites in Egypt. Some Jews regard the hidden half as symbolizing the Messiah, the "hidden one," who will bring about the final redemption. The child "steals" the matzoh and holds it for ransom, and the seder cannot end until it is eaten.

You don't have to be Jewish to appreciate how the Passover seder fosters interaction, mutual respect, and a bond with the Divine among those who participate. Observant Jews keep a

Tibetan and Navajo life is a process of constant rebalancing and perfecting of one's actions, expressions, and thoughts into an ideal state as befits each culture's ultimate role models. . . . Both groups see the process of living as a spiritual journey, an individual and communal effort to develop each person into the best version of him or herself, in the company of likeminded people dedicated to the integration of matter and spirit.

— Peter Gold,
Navajo and Tibetan Sacred Wisdom

kosher kitchen, one that obeys the laws set forth for them in the Torah. The great lesson of this is that those who would keep a sacred kitchen should value a sense of commitment, the practicing of ritual symbolizing a living connection to the Divine, and joy in the formerly mundane tasks of cooking and serving dinner.

A symbolic meal is found in many cultures, as is the place set for a spiritual guest, and meanings ascribed to various parts of the meal. You can adapt principles from the seder to your own religious celebration, as in for example, the Sacred Kitchen Consecration ceremony that follows and in the Feast of Light celebration described in chapter 6.

PRAYERS, BLESSINGS, AND CONSECRATION

Whatever your religious faith, introducing a blessing of the food and a prayer of thanks before a meal is a powerful way to extend the sacred kitchen from stove top to table. It is a way of praising the higher power, Yahweh, Allah, God — all names for the Supreme Being, the Eternal Radiance, the provider of the life force to all living beings. Blessings are a way of thanking God the Father and Mother not only for our food, but for every aspect of our lives. They provide a simple way to acknowledge our connection to the Creator and to all people. Through prayer, we keep the spark of our own divinity alive, even beneath the weight of life's pressures and distractions.

"The highest form of prayer," writes author Charles Panati in *Sacred Origins of Profound Things*, "consists of contemplation of God himself. It is the kind of intense meditation we most accurately associate with the prayers of mystics, and it's the purest form of prayer. We ask no favors; we just adore our Creator."

However you define prayer, something mystical and powerful happens when you deliberately engage God's ear with deep conviction and sanctify your meal through the radiance, sincerity, and vibrations of your voice. Whether it is a simple blessing or an elaborate ritual, you can bring a sense of peace and love to your meal time by saying the words with intent and sincerity. Partaking of the

The Great Invocation

From the point of Light
within the Mind of God
Let light stream forth into
the minds of men.
Let Light descend on Earth.

From the point of Love
within the Heart of God
Let love stream forth into
the hearts of men.
May Christ return to Earth.

From the center where
the Will of God is known
Let purpose guide the
little wills of men —
To purpose which the
Masters know and serve.

From the center which
we call the race of men
Let the Plan of Love and
Light work out
And may it seal the door
where evil dwells.

Let Light and Love and
Power restore the
Plan on Earth.

meal can become a form of meditation, a galvanizing factor for your home members, and a way of receiving the gifts of the life force with gratitude.

Panati points out that the Bible shows we didn't begin praying until after Eve's grandson Seth was born: "At that time men began to call upon the name of the Lord." (Genesis 4:26) Other, more ancient religions, however, show that humankind has been praying for a very long time indeed.

Wherever you worship, prayers tend to fall into one of five categories:

- Adoration
- Confession
- Petition
- Praise
- Thanksgiving

The blessing of a meal can use any combination of these, but thanksgiving should be included in every case. Whether for a religious holiday or just Thursday-night dinner, by voicing a blessing we consecrate a meal or gathering to a meaningful purpose. In the words we utter, we invoke care and blessings from the Divine for ourselves and those around us. We also praise and acknowledge divine magnanimity and solicit protection or favor. With a blessing, we can actually make the meal holy, if we believe it to be so, and venerate the Divine within each other as we dine.

In *The Rituals of Dinner*, author Margaret Visser tells us: "An ancient Christian custom accompanying grace was the host's marking with a cross the round bread-loaf that was about to be shared. Prayer may end the meal, as it commonly does in Jewish practice." She goes on to say that Moslems begin meals by saying "*Bismil'lah!*" ("In God's name!") as they roll back their right sleeves to eat. They declare "*Hamdallah!*" ("Praise be to God!") on completion of the meal. Through prayer, you can consecrate your kitchen, and dedicate it to the sacred purposes of nourishing and healing.

The Sacred Kitchen points the way toward an understanding of the life force in food, how chi flows through you and your kitchen, and the importance of centeredness in both your diet and your mind. You have also seen some of the ways in which various religions use ritual and ceremony to make abstract philosophical ideas concrete. We can think ourselves as being close to the Creator while performing four specific acts: during prayer, while meditating, while making love, and while eating. So why shouldn't we consecrate our kitchen work space and our food through mindfulness every time we cook?

With cures for proper chi flow in place, along with symbols of sacredness that have meaning to you, you can dedicate your sacred kitchen with the following simple ceremony. After you have gathered together a new white candle, a stick of incense, some salt, and a piece of bread, assemble those who wish to participate. Ask those present to clear their thoughts and be mindful that this consecration will declare the kitchen and its function sacred from this point forward. Next, an elected leader reads the following benediction:

> We gather to consecrate this sacred kitchen and dedicate it to health and sustenance, God's life-giving gift to us all. May we enter the kitchen with reverence for its miracles and with respect for those who cook here.
>
> (Light the candle and sprinkle a few grains of salt into everyone's hands.)
>
> With this flame we commemorate our centeredness in mind and body to the flame of centeredness in the heart of God. With this salt we keep mindful that we are the salt of the earth, and that as we quiet our minds, we shall be spiritually nourished whenever we take time to listen to the Lord.
>
> (Each person takes a pinch of the bread and eats.)
>
> This bread reminds us that through the Father-Mother God we shall never go hungry. We shall work to share nature's bounty in gratitude with those who don't have enough to eat.

With all beings and all things we shall be as relatives.

— Black Elk, Oglala Sioux holy man

(Light the incense.)

We invoke the Holy Spirit to consecrate this sacred space, to nourish and heal everyone who eats in our house. Amen.

The Lord's Prayer

Our Father who art in heaven,
Hallowed be Thy Name,
Thy kingdom come,
Thy will be done,
On earth, as it is in heaven.
Give us this day our daily bread
And forgive us our trespasses,
As we forgive those who trespass against us.
And lead us not into temptation,
But deliver us from evil;
For thine is the kingdom,
And the power, and the glory, for ever.
Amen.

— Jesus, Matthew 6:9–13

Whenever you dine, have the host or a child say grace. When alone, utter out loud a prayer of gratitude and blessing on the meal. Remember that blessing the meal and praising the Creator who provided it honors the sacred kitchen and also honors the miraculous activity of the cook who prepared and served it.

LA NUEVA HORA DE LA FAMILIA

In our sacred kitchen, we want to convey the life force from the garden to the mixing bowl, to the stove top, and finally to the table, where the act of eating is elevated to bring meaning and healing to our lives. We can make a great start simply by adding blessings and ritual periodically at mealtime.

You will find that the best new traditions can be found in the old ones. What is your own ethnic background or nationality? If you have lost touch, ask grandparents or other members of your extended family to supply details. If there are no family members to ask, you can research your background through the library or genealogy. Failing that, you can start from scratch, creating your own family traditions based on the above gleanings from the world's sacred customs.

For example, you can research the symbology of every aspect of the Passover seder or adapt ideas from other religions. Base new customs on your own religious ideals, and find scriptural teachings and prayers by which you can invoke blessings from and express gratitude to the Creator. Above all, give everyone in attendance a role to play. It doesn't have to take more than a moment or two. In this way, you can create a personal celebration for yourself. Give the ritual a purpose, and then build meaningful practices around it.

If you have a family, show them that there is satisfaction and meaning in the preparation of food, and that they are touching the Creator through the enjoyment of eating. Make cooking a household necessity, explaining to your loved ones how important it is and why you are suddenly "making such a big deal" out of dinner. It might mean more to them if they feel they have played a role in bringing the food to the table and in choosing the elements of the ritual. A century ago, the household's survival demanded that everyone contribute, even the youngest child. It made each one feel responsible and valuable.

Propose a new weekly or monthly family hour — we call it *La Nueva Hora de la Familia,* even though we are not Spanish speakers. And there's a reason. The makeup of American society itself is quietly changing. Within the next ten years, Hispanic Americans will outnumber African Americans. Not only that, but around the same time, nonwhites will outnumber whites. Everyone in the wonderful melting pot of the United States must acknowledge this, either by applying the principles of wisdom, love, and community, or through mistakes such as violence, hatred, and segregation. The choice is up to us, as individuals, as neighborhoods, communities, and as a

Let all who are hungry come and eat; let all who are in need come share our Passover.

— The *ha lahma anya*, Passover blessing

nation. By necessity, we will all be bilingual, but eventually we must also realize our oneness as children of God and as American citizens. We shouldn't destroy the traditions that define our ethnic diversity, but we would all benefit by discovering and sharing some new traditions that will help to unify and strengthen us.

For use with everyday meals, print out a dedication, a blessing, and a word of thanks and keep them handy near the table. Be flexible, and keep it simple so you can't use lack of time as an excuse. For a weekly or monthly celebration, write down some specific steps based on the universal themes that emerge in most of the world's sacred traditions. Here are some of the most often used elements.

Many religious customs involve cleaning the house and fasting to clean the body and clear the mind. Chinese people clean house prior to the Spring Festival, Colombians prior to Easter, and Jews prior to Passover. Many Christians fast during Lent (the forty-day period prior to Easter) and cleaning is a symbolic ritual in many Christian countries.

So, let the act of cleaning be a part of the holy work that takes place in your home. Incorporate customs that will help you feel closer to God, and let the entire household participate in choosing and practicing them. In this way, you can make every day holy and something to look forward to. Highlight certain days that coincide with your personal religious beliefs, and choose special dishes that you will make only at that time.

Here are some more themes and customs to consider as you choose elements for your daily, weekly, monthly, or yearly celebrations. The faithful among the world's religious traditions:

- Give thanks and bless the food.
- Incorporate prayers of praise, forgiveness, and gratitude.
- Invite a saint, angel, or prophet to join them (set a place).
- Light seven candles in some pleasing configuration (Kwanzaa, Hanukah).
- Serve bread as a symbolic food.
  Recite special prayers or blessings.

Enhance your traditions by adding meaningful festive elements. These can provide other benefits, such as more quality time to spend with loved ones, or just plain fun:

- Put on new clothes for the day.
- Clean house.
- Plant a garden.
- Harvest vegetables.
- Prepare special foods.

The Sacred Kitchen urges everyone to incorporate a family hour into each household to help us all feel more at peace with ourselves and with each other. In the next chapter, we're going to get into the spirit by making dinner together. We'll also look at how our supermarket and kitchen choices affect the health of the planet, and celebrate the world's most universal spiritual theme in a new ceremony called the Feast of Light.

RECIPES FOR NEW TRADITIONS

In the spirit of global unity for all God's people, we have carefully selected some recipes from various cultures. These dishes combine to make a complete new meal, delicious and meaningful in its own right, and expressing an ancient teaching: "The paths are many, the truth is one."

In many cultures, two people do not feel they can talk in a friendly way with each other unless they have first eaten together: it is an equivalent of being "properly introduced." A corresponding attitude is that which makes it impossible for a desert Arab who has once eaten salt with a man ever to treat him thereafter as an enemy. It is as though reconciliation must never be needed, because it has taken place already; enmity has been overcome in advance.

— Margaret Visser, in *The Rituals of Dinner*

Harira (Ramadan Soup)

A satisfying, restorative soup is always part of Eid al-Fitr, the feast following the days of fasting of Ramadan, but it's also a great way to begin most any meal.

1 tablespoon canola oil
1 large onion, chopped
$3/4$ cup dried lentils
$3/4$ cup rice
8 cups water
1 cup diced tomatoes
2 cups cooked chickpeas
$1/4$ cup chopped fresh parsley
2 tablespoons fresh lemon juice
Salt and freshly ground pepper to taste

Heat the oil in a large soup pot over medium heat. Add the onion, cover, and cook until the onion is softened, about 5 minutes. Add the lentils, rice, water, and tomatoes and bring to a boil. Reduce heat to low, cover, and simmer for 30 minutes. Add all the remaining ingredients. Simmer, uncovered, for 10 minutes. Taste and adjust the seasoning.

Serves 6

HOPPIN' JOHN

A tradition in the American South, Hoppin' John is traditionally eaten on New Year's Day for good luck. It follows that it would be included in a Kwanzaa feast since they occur at the same time. To compliment the meal, serve with a bowl of cooked collards, kale, or other dark, leafy greens.

1 tablespoon canola oil
1 large onion, finely chopped
2 garlic cloves, minced
16 ounces dried black-eyed peas
3 cups Vital Vegetable Stock (page 172)
$1/4$ teaspoon red pepper flakes
$1 1/2$ cups long-grain rice
8 ounces vegetarian sausage, crumbled
Salt and freshly ground pepper to taste

Heat the oil in a large saucepan over medium heat. Add the onion, cover, and cook until softened, about 5 minutes. Remove cover, add the garlic and cook until fragrant, about 30 seconds. Stir in the black-eyed peas, the stock, 1 cup water, and the red pepper flakes, and bring to a boil. Reduce heat to low, cover, and simmer 45 to 50 minutes, or until peas are tender. In a saucepan, combine the rice and 3 cups of water, cover, and bring to a boil. Reduce heat to low and simmer for 20 to 30 minutes, or until rice is tender. While peas and rice are cooking, brown the vegetarian sausage in a skillet over medium heat and set aside. In a large bowl combine the hot cooked rice, the browned vegetarian sausage, and the cooked black-eyed peas. Season with salt and pepper and serve.

Serves 4 to 6

An Essene Blessing

When the natural seasons come,
at whatever time may be;
When, too, the months begin;
on their feasts and on holy days,
as they come in order due,
each as a memorial in its season —
I shall hold it as one of the laws
Engraven of old on the tablets
To render to God as my tribute
— the blessings of my lips.

— from The Hymn of the Initiates, Dead Sea Scrolls

HAROSET

This chutneylike seder relish is delicious any time of the year. The sweet-tart flavor can be altered to suit your own taste. It complements the flavors of Hoppin' John.

$1/2$ cup raisins
3 tablespoons dry red wine or apple juice
2 green apples, peeled, cored, and chopped
$1/2$ cup chopped walnuts
1 tablespoon packed brown sugar
1 teaspoon ground cinnamon

Put the raisins and wine or juice in a small bowl and soak for at least 1 hour. Put the apples, walnuts, sugar, cinnamon, and soaked raisins, and liquid in a blender or food processor and pulse to combine. The texture should be slightly chunky, so be careful not to over process. Transfer to a small bowl and refrigerate until serving time.

Makes about 2 $1/2$ cups

STICKY RICE BALLS (TANG YUAN)

When made from scratch, sticky rice balls can take the whole day to make. Fortunately, they are available pre-made in the freezer section of Asian markets. The round shape symbolized perfection and is an important shape in Chinese culture. This sublime dessert is part of the Chinese New Year feast.

3 cups water
1 package frozen sticky rice balls

Put the water in a saucepan and bring to a boil over high heat. Reduce heat to medium, add the rice balls, and simmer for about

2 minutes, being careful not to overcook. Put the balls in individual serving bowls, pour a small amount of the cooking liquid over each, and serve hot.

Serves 4

Grace Before Meals
(The traditional Roman Catholic blessing)

Bless us, Oh Lord,
And these Thy gifts,
Which we are about to receive
From Thy bounty,
Through Christ Our Lord, Amen.

6

The Sacred Kitchen Experience

*My kitchen is a mystical place, a kind of temple for me. It is
a place where the surfaces seem to have significance,
where the sounds and odors carry meaning that
transfers from the past and bridges to the future.*

— Pearl Bailey, *Pearl's Kitchen*

The sacred kitchen comes alive in all its richness, beauty, and power when tasks are performed mindfully and linked with the Divine in celebration. But did you know that you and your kitchen are a powerful force in the world beyond your home, in your community, and on the planet itself? We now explore this idea and then help to make the sacred kitchen become a reality in your home by making dinner together. We also introduce a new universal celebration — The Feast of Light — that embraces a theme common to every religious faith. Finally, we see how higher-consciousness cooking can lead us to greater happiness in our noncooking lives.

A crust eaten in peace is better than a banquet partaken in anxiety.

— Aesop

FEEDING THE MULTITUDE

In chapter 5, we explored the role food plays in the world's religious feasts. It was noted that several of the miracles performed by Jesus of Nazareth involved food in some way. It may surprise you to know that the story of the loaves and fishes miracle can add an important ingredient to higher-consciousness cooking and a personal connection to our brothers and sisters around the world.

After the murder of John the Baptist at Herod's infamous banquet, the mood in Capernaum had become unstable and dangerous, both for Jesus and His disciples as well as for the people in Herod's jurisdiction. Jesus resolved to leave Capernaum immediately so as to diffuse an uprising. With the people's safety in mind, and the disciples' need for rest, He sailed across Lake Galilee to a place six miles away inside the jurisdiction of the Tetrarch Philip.

It was a beautiful spring day, and it had been a long one. But there would be no rest, as people had run along the edge of the lake, fording the Jordan two miles upstream, in order to meet Jesus and his disciples on their arrival. In no time, the crowd grew to more than five thousand. They included John's heartbroken followers from Capernaum as well as pilgrims on their way to Jerusalem to observe Passover.

Jesus and His followers were reclining on a hilltop talking, when He was overcome with intense compassion for the thousands who were gathering around him. He descended the hill to greet them and began teaching and healing those in need.

By afternoon, the crowd was hungry. The disciples urged the Nazarene to send the people away so they could find something to eat, but Jesus said, "*You* give them something to eat." They had with them the equivalent of about fifteen dollars and asked if they should purchase bread with it. Jesus asked how much bread they had, and they told him five loaves, along with two fishes. He then had the people sit on the ground. He took the loaves and fishes in hand and looked up to heaven, gave thanks, and broke the bread, miraculously producing enough food not only to feed the people, but to fill twelve baskets of leftovers.

The principle exemplified by Jesus' feeding of the multitude

Feeding the Multitude

Then Jesus called his disciples to him and said, "I have compassion on the crowd, because they have been with me now three days, and have nothing to eat; and I am unwilling to send them away hungry, lest they faint on the way." And the disciples said to him, "Where are we to get bread enough in the desert to feed so great a crowd?" And Jesus said to them, "How many loaves have you?" They said, "Seven, and a few small fish." And commanding the crowd to sit down on the ground, he took the seven loaves and the fish, and having given thanks, he broke them and gave them to the disciples, and the disciples gave them to the crowds. And they all ate and were satisfied; and they took up seven baskets full of the broken pieces leftover. Those who ate were four thousand men, besides women and children. — Matthew 15:32–38

reflects various aspects of the holy work we do in the sacred kitchen. We are reminded of the alchemy of cooking and how every meal is greater than the sum of its parts — whether we are baking a loaf of bread, making soup, or tossing a summer salad.

The feeding of the multitude reminds us of how we ourselves convey divine energy into food when we cook. Our chi, colored by our moods, joins the life force in the food we are preparing. When performed with love and compassion, we amplify the Divine in any meal. We are also reminded of how compassion is the great healer, not only of ourselves, but of those we feed.

We all know miracles when we see them. In 1998, a two-year-old child in Georgia, blown to the top of a tree by a tornado, was rescued without a scratch. Lone survivors have been discovered in the rubble of plane crashes. People with hopeless illnesses have been known to experience sudden, inexplicable cures. But feeding a multitude? That one occurred in a quiet neighborhood in South Carolina after Hurricane Hugo.

HEALING BY HURRICANE

During the 1980s, when the authors lived in Charleston, South Carolina, Robin worked with a chef named Martin Flannery.

A highly skilled and talented chef, Martin was intrinsically quiet and withdrawn. He hid behind a tough professional demeanor that instilled fear and respect in all who worked for him. He ran his kitchen with discipline and precision.

Like many restaurant professionals, Martin worked long, grueling hours, from early morning until late evening, often seven days a week. The kitchen was his life and his life was the kitchen. Although he had a wife and a daughter at home in a Charleston suburb, he rarely saw them. His social interactions were limited to barking at the wait staff, reprimanding the cooks, and ordering ingredients from food purveyors. His reserved personality was often put to the test by admiring patrons who asked to meet him — a duty his shyness made unbearable.

In September 1989, Charleston became ground zero for Hurricane Hugo, which wiped out homes and businesses on the barrier islands and knocked out power and phone lines to the entire area for weeks. With the city in a shambles, restaurants couldn't open, so life as Martin knew it stopped cold. Now, the unfamiliar territory of his own home replaced the stainless steel safety and fluorescent lights of his restaurant kitchen haven.

Once the winds died down, the morning sun rose on his neighborhood to reveal a war zone. With his neighbors, he ventured outside into the cul-de-sac to survey the damage. Trees and debris were strewn everywhere. Among the fallen limbs and downed wires, he faced his neighbors for the first time. Suddenly Martin was thrust into an unavoidable social interaction. The laborious cleanup stretched throughout that endless first day. The all-electric neighborhood grew dark and silent, and children and adults alike complained that they were hungry.

That's when a strange thing happened. While others stood by helplessly wondering what to do, Martin quietly took charge. Painfully determined, he dragged his barbecue grill out to the center of the cul-de-sac. With little diplomacy, he ordered his neighbors to do the same.

"Bring your grills out here," he snapped with the same finesse he used for his kitchen staff. "Line them up with mine and bring out any food that's going to spoil." Perplexed, the neighbors obeyed. He fired up all the grills, side by side, and cooked gourmet-quality food all evening for the great multitude that had gathered.

During the dark, frustrating days that followed, before power was restored and life could return to normal, Martin was seen in the center of his neighborhood manning the semi-circle of grills — inadvertently bringing the neighbors together and creating a sense of community with people he had rarely spoken to.

Circumstances beyond his control had forced Martin to break free from his own limitations. Through compassion, he had used his professional skills for the nurturing of others, bringing sanity to the chaos of his neighborhood through cooking. After Hugo, Martin returned to the hectic safety of his restaurant. He didn't change his manner much, but though he rarely spoke personally about himself to Robin, he seemed more open. She observed that his edges were softer in social situations and that something inside him had healed.

Hopefully, we'll never face the circumstances that brought Martin Flannery out of his shell, but our kitchens, and the choices we make in them, play a vital role in the arenas of pollution and world hunger. Though we won't be required to divide the loaves and fishes, the feeding of the multitudes is a responsibility shared by everyone who has more than they need. This is because our purchases, attitudes, and compassion, though we live far away from the agonies of developing nations, can have a direct effect throughout the world. Our choice is whether that effect is deleterious or miraculous.

EXPANDING YOUR CIRCLE OF AWARENESS

Martin Flannery's story is a perfect example of how we can apply spiritual practice meaningfully in our kitchen work. The principle is emphasized by "food missionary" Ron Pickarski in *Eco-Cuisine*, in which he takes the idea one step further: "Spiritual practice cannot be detached from practical action. One of the most practical issues is ecology." Can you really scrub your organic carrots for the good of all? The answer is yes, and here's why.

> Love is feeding everybody.
>
> — John Denver

From the unreal lead me
to the real!
From darkness lead me
to light!
From death lead me to
immortality!

— A Hindu prayer

What we do in the kitchen affects the world's resources and health beginning with our every purchase at the grocery store. Wherever we spend our money and whatever we spend it on casts a measurable vote for the product, all its components, packaging, and advertising, and the actions of the company that makes it. We vote "yes" for the entire chain of processes that goes into producing food and disposing of its waste products. These votes, which we cast on a daily basis at the store, are more powerful than the votes we cast in a political election. Every cook needs to realize that this can work to our mutual advantage: We take power away from polluters and environmental exploiters simply by making intentional choices with planetary compassion when we shop.

Mother Nature's limitless pantry is always open, and the world is her all-you-can-eat buffet. The light of the Father's creative spirit inspires her unending generosity to feed and nourish the peoples of the world. But starvation, arising out of poverty, drought, and war, is inexcusable on a planet where wealthy nations have more food than they can use and possess the technology and resources to solve all but the most severe of natural catastrophes.

Chapter 4 underscored the nutritional wisdom of a grain-based diet from historical, ethical, and medical viewpoints, but the environmental impact of meat products should also be a consideration in the sacred kitchen.

News sources are stingy with the full story about the depletion of the rain forests. We know that they are being destroyed one football field per second in order to produce food, but what is not generally known is that most of the food isn't for people: The land is being cleared to create grazing land for beef cattle, which will in turn provide a continuous source of inexpensive meat for American fast-food restaurants. Fast-food companies import beef from developing countries who use their precious farmland to supply America with cheap burgers, instead of growing healthful grains for their own starving people. It takes sixteen pounds of grain and twenty-five hundred gallons of water to produce one pound of meat, but sixteen people would be fed on the grain it takes to create that pound of meat. Producing that grain requires only 250 gallons of water.

Add to this the sobering fact that every two seconds a human child starves to death, and we can see that the emergence of a centered cuisine is essential in developed countries in the new millennium. As people everywhere wake up to the realities of our unwise dietary habits of the past, the sacred kitchen is already taking hold. In keeping with the healing and harmony brought forth in centeredness, therefore, we urge that everyone consider extending the circle of awareness to the use of cruelty-free and biodegradable products.

Some people even take the idea of shopping wisely for world welfare to the level of activism: making every purchase count in the neighborhood, community, and the world at large. The reach of the sacred kitchen knows no bounds.

A FAIR SHARE

Few of us will be confronted with feeding a throng of pilgrims in the desert, but we approach just such a miracle when we deliberately play a part to end starvation in the world. We can do this by encouraging government to continue sharing technology and surplus foods wherever starvation exists. We can also support world hunger organizations, some addresses for which are listed in Appendix II: Resources Directory, along with other humanitarian organizations. One of the best examples of someone who puts her sacred kitchen beliefs into action worldwide is a Philadelphia phenomenon named Judy Wicks.

Wicks is a restaurateur, eco-businesswoman, and international activist for human rights. She started her White Dog Café in Philadelphia in 1983 on the first floor of her home, where the kitchen was a charcoal grill in the backyard, and customers had to use the bathroom upstairs in her living quarters. A conscientious hippie in her youth, she now seats two hundred in the White Dog, has a retail store, and employs one hundred people. She serves organic produce from local family farms and humanely raised animal products — and she deeply believes that this matters.

She is also vice chair of Social Venture Network, a national organization of over four hundred business owners and social entrepreneurs dedicated to using business as a vehicle for creating a just and sustainable society. These entrepreneurs are dedicated to buying local, supporting family and minority vendors, and pro-

> We have the know-it-all to feed everybody, clothe everybody, give every human on earth a chance. We dwell instead on petty things. . . . What a waste of time. Think of it. What a chance we have."
>
> — R. Buckminster Fuller

moting other like-minded businesses in their communities.

As she stated in a speech delivered in Havana, Cuba, in June 1998, Wicks's business philosophy is based on the realization that "a successful and sustainable economy is not one based on hoarding, but on sharing; not on excluding, but on finding a way for everyone to play the game according to their individual strengths and interests."

The White Dog hosts many nontraditional celebrations, such as the Native American Thanksgiving Dinner, Noche Latina, and a Freedom Seder. It also celebrates birthdays for Dr. Martin Luther King, Jr., and Mahatma Gandhi. Each fall, the restaurant honors organic gardening with a Dance of the Ripe Tomatoes.

"I once had a vision of walking into a restaurant," she says, "and instead of asking for a table for two or for four, I said, 'Table for 6 billion, please!'™ — a seat for everyone in the world, a world where everyone not only has enough to eat, but also a world in which everyone has a place at the table, both politically and economically."

Wicks has been accused of using food to lure customers into social activism, because she arranges trips for her customers to dine at "sister restaurants" in places such as Mexico, Vietnam, and Indonesia. She once organized a business group to help the embattled indigenous coffee farmers in Chiapas, Mexico.

This type of international awareness in the form of multicultural, community supportive, health-conscious entrepreneurship is growing. But you may ask, "What can I do from my little kitchen that would help?"

International activism may not be high on your to-do list this year, but there are plenty of things you can do that positively effect the quality of life for everyone. As Mahatma Gandhi once said, "Whatever you do may seem insignificant, but it is very important that you do it!"

Our tendency is to limit our concentration only to those things that touch us directly. We often don't have time to do more than nod when some world tragedy gets its fifteen-second mention on the six o'clock news.

But your practice in the sacred kitchen is now mindful. The space itself has a harmonious flow of chi, and you have a new-found reverence for the spiritual sources of foodstuffs. A breakfast as simple as coffee and toast is honored with a prayer and thanks for the privilege and the miracle that brought it to the table. You use meals to honor higher principles of your religious beliefs or household triumphs and successes. As you cook, you are one with at least a billion other people cooking at the same time. We can honor them through the products we buy and avoid. We can support them by supporting organizations and government programs that promote training and share food with nations whose people do not have enough to eat.

Eighteenth-century British political thinker Edmund Burke once said, "Nobody made a greater mistake than he who did nothing because he could only do a little."

So here are a few things that you can do that will have a tremendous impact as more people practice the principles of a sacred kitchen:

- Buy foods that are made from natural products.
- Buy biodegradable products from companies that do not test on animals.
- Avoid products that pollute, are toxic, or are contrary to maximum health.
- Every grocery shopping trip, buy a can of vegetables or a bag of grain to donate to a hunger program — less than a dollar per week.
- Shop with canvas or net bags — plastic doesn't break down,

If one offers Me with
love and devotion a leaf,
a flower, fruit, or water, I
will accept it.

— Bhagavad-Gita (9:26)

and paper wastes trees.

- Snip six-pack rings (wildlife gets trapped in them).
- Recycle cans, glass, paper: It decreases our trash, saves energy and resources, preserves natural habitats, conserves water, and reduces air pollution.
- Aerate your faucets to use less water.
- Eat a centered cuisine: Eating lower on the food chain can end world hunger. Over a billion people could be fed by the grain and soybeans eaten by U.S. livestock every year.
- Compost vegetable waste and return it to your garden.

We are all responsible for hunger in the world, especially when farmers receive low prices for producing a bumper crop, as occurred nationally in 1998. Write your congresspersons to divert some wasted revenues into buying and distributing surplus foods to starving nations. Demand that we train armies, not for war, but to teach self-sustaining technologies to developing countries. Insist that a segment of the country's economy be kept strong by funding international education programs such as the Peace Corps, UNICEF, the Food and Agriculture Organization, and many others (see Appendix II: Resources Directory).

Contribute to your community and church pantry programs to make even a small regular contribution for the hungry of the world. Donate to local homeless shelters, soup kitchens, and to any program in your area that sponsors food drives, whether for the starving of the world, or for disaster relief.

Nineteenth-century transcendental poet Ralph Waldo Emerson once said, "To give of one's self; to leave the world a bit better, whether by a healthy child, a garden patch, or a redeemed social condition . . . to know that even one life has breathed easier because you have lived — this is to have succeeded." Sharing is the heart of the sacred kitchen. The cook is the instrument through which the Creator's good energy passes in order to heal all who would partake of a centered diet.

Every nation is a potential altruist in times of plenty, and potentially the one in need in times of disaster. But one way or another, we are responsible stewards of Mother Nature's larder.

How is it that one nation can idly sit by while another starves?

The late sixties activist Abbie Hoffman once said that activism had been little reported in the media since the shootings at Kent State in 1970. This is still true, save for the occasional Greenpeace demonstration that interferes with military vessels, or a People for the Ethical Treatment of Animals (PETA) anti-fur campaign for which the beautiful and famous remove their clothes. But according to a host of environmental organizations and ecology-related magazines, activism is quietly alive and well in communities throughout the United States. *Orion Afield* magazine, published by the Orion Society, Great Barrington, Massachusetts, shows in its Autumn 1998 issue that this is occurring, and with increasing support from mainstream religion.

In 1996, the U.S. Catholic Conference published a parish resource called *Let the Earth Bless the Lord: God's Creation and Our Responsibility*, which gives advice for promoting environmental justice. The publication reported that groups such as Mothers of East L.A. are typical of parishes forming grassroots community organizations that tackle issues such as environmental injustice head on. The women of various Los Angeles parishes have worked together to successfully oppose a waste incinerator near their community and also to prevent a chemical plant from being built near a local high school. They use prayer as one of their strongest allies in getting things done.

Ecosattva, a group of environmentally aware activists from the Buddhist Peace Fellowship at Green Gulch Farm, Sausalito, California, work on various ecological issues in northern California including, most recently, opposing the logging of old-growth redwoods. To them, standing up for environmental issues is part of their boddhisattva vow to benefit all beings. The cutting of the redwoods was also opposed by a Jewish group that publishes the *Coalition on the Environment and Jewish Life* newsletter. Pressure from Jewish activists has opened a channel of communication with the corporate executive who controls the unprotected redwood forest in North America.

The Summer 1997 issue of the Evangelical Environmental Network's *Green Cross* reports that the Franciscan environmental

> Now I can look at you in peace; I don't eat you anymore.
>
> — Franz Kafka, said to a fish in an aquarium

Nothing would be more tiresome than eating and drinking if God had not made them a pleasure as well as a necessity.

—Voltaire

justice organization called the Southwest Environmental Equity Project (Sweep) works in northern Mexico, where the population has increased more than ten times in a few years due to the relocation of U.S. factories as the result of NAFTA. They use the principles of Francis of Assisi's love of creation and concern for the poor in getting things done. They work with people who suffer from illness caused by environmental pollutants. Says activist Bonnie Danowski, "I think people are starting to see that human health is connected to the health of the environment."

The Orion Society is dedicated to supporting changes in ethics and action at the local level, that offer solutions to the environmental crises through cultivating nature literacy. Its magazine, *Orion Afield*, keeps like-minded communities informed on subjects such as the "local currency" movement, in which communities are printing and using their own scrip as a means of local exchange. They also report on trends in "localism," in which communities succeed in reducing their dependence on the global economy by creating sustainable local enterprises, as well as education, conservation, and restoration.

Grassroots religious organizations are incorporating environmental issues into their ethical and spiritual foundations of justice and world health. In October 1998, ten conferences on religions of the world and ecology were sponsored in New York City by the Harvard University Center for the Study of World Religions. Participants explored the common ground of religion and ecology, making a report to the United Nations with its findings. The entire series will be published by Harvard University Press in 1999.

Use your sacred kitchen principles in your local community environment. Find out what the environmental issues are in your area, and play a role, however involved or limited. Bring food charged in your kitchen with your own hands and offer it to the community as a blessing for success in improving conditions where you live. Bring some food to the PTA, and serve something wonderful at any community potluck where centered food can inspire people to reexamine their dietary habits and look for a better way to live.

Finally, be sure to share your recipes, your knowledge, and

any other talents that you can add. Helen Caldicott, M.D., Australian physician, anti-nuclear activist, and founder of International Physicians to Save the Environment, writes in her book *If You Love This Planet: A Plan to Heal the Earth*, "Only if we understand the beauty of nature will we love it, and only if we become alerted to learn about the planet's disease processes can we decide to live our lives with a proper sense of ecological responsibility." Caldicott believes that "Only if we love nature, learn about its ills, and live accordingly will we be inspired to participate in needed legislative activities to save the earth. So my prescription for action to save the planet is Love, learn, live, and legislate."

The importance of our interconnectedness and dependency on each other's sense of environmental responsibility cannot be overstated. Nor can the importance of the spirit of sharing when we enter the temple of our sacred kitchen to work with God's gift of food. Farmers grow the food. Stores distribute it. Eating our daily bread is a process that requires our awareness and participation. Without that spirit of sharing, we create our own hell, as an ancient story from Jewish folklore perfectly exemplifies.

Once there was a rabbi who wanted to see both heaven and hell. After much pleading, God finally agreed to grant him his wish. In a moment, the rabbi was standing before a large, blank door. As the door began to open, he became afraid, but soon found himself standing in a crowded hall festively decorated for a banquet. A large table was heaped with succulent and sumptuous food that had driven the people into a frenzy of appetite. They were seated around the table holding long, strange spoons. They were sobbing and crying out from hunger, the delicious food just waiting to be eaten. The rabbi thought it such a horrible place as he watched them trying to feed themselves. The spoons God had given to them were too long. They could not reach their mouths to eat no matter how they tried to stretch their arms. The sobbing people were starving, even though the food was ready to eat. The rabbi suddenly knew he was in hell, and as the knowledge dawned on him, the door closed.

He shut his eyes and immediately began to pray, begging God to take him far away from that awful place. But when he opened

> The soul is light, the mind is light, and the body is light — light of different grades; and it is this relation which connects man with the planets and stars.
>
> — Aphorisms from *The Sufi Message* by Hinayat Inayat Khan

his eyes, he thought God had not answered his prayers, for he was standing in front of the same door. The door creaked open once again, revealing the same room as before.

However, just before he turned away in horror, he saw that the same people seated around the same table, holding the same long spoons were no longer sobbing. Instead of crying out, they were blessing the food and thanking God, as they used the long spoons *to feed each other.*

Once the rabbi heard them praising God, the door once again shut before him. He prayed again, this time in thanks that God had shown him the meaning of heaven and hell, and the slight change in attitude that made all the difference between them. The length of the spoons had not changed, but the people who couldn't see beyond their selfish desires had created hell for themselves, whereas those who sought to feed others found themselves in heaven.

We can spend more of our time in heaven, right here on earth, when we are in the kitchen, by remembering our connection to the global kitchen — to everyone cooking at the same time, in the never-ending wave of breakfast, lunch, and dinner initiated by the continuous rising of the sun. As such, let every act, product, and discard be regarded as a contribution to the general welfare of the planet and her people. Even if you perform only a few of the following actions every week, your hands will join other hands perpetually engaged in feeding the multitudes of the earth and caring for our planet sensibly. Whenever you cook, try to:

- Shop locally.
- Support minority businesses.
- Avoid using plastics as containers or bags.
- Support international food organizations.
- Recycle.
- Compost vegetable wastes for your backyard garden.
- Limit or eliminate use of animal products.

Keeping in mind the planet friendly principles above, let's cook a meal together. Not just any meal, but one that is tailor-made for new traditions that you may introduce in your home. As we cook, we'll also track the higher meaning of what we experience along the way.

MAKING A CELEBRATION DINNER

Let's share a sacred experience together by making dinner — what we call the Celebration Dinner. For this dinner, we have chosen four recipes that are easy to make, but which exemplify the principles of *The Sacred Kitchen.* This meal is ideal for any celebration in which food plays a central role. For other celebratory dinners, you can adapt the recipes, use others in this book, or use recipes of your own to add personal significance.

The first recipe, Potage du Soleil, truly a "soup of the sun," is a delicate blending of yellow summer squash, creamy oat milk, and rich almond butter. This pale yellow soup is garnished with sunflower seeds, which lend a surprising crunch to the velvety texture. Potage du Soleil is a delicious way to begin any meal.

The main course of our dinner is Celebration Salmagundi. It symbolizes global unity, the bringing together of varied components to create a unified whole. In addition, it is filled with a bounty of fresh vegetables and is brimming with vital nutrients. It is served over Eight-Treasure Rice, a vibrant and flavorful rice pilaf.

The final course of the Celebration Dinner is called Create-Your-Own-Reality Sundaes. Much more than a typical ice cream sundae, this dessert involves group participation, sharing, and creativity. It's also fun to make and delicious to eat. The table is set with serving bowls of nondairy frozen dessert, sorbet (or frozen yogurt or ice cream, if you prefer), fresh fruit, fruit toppings, ground nuts, and other toppings. Everyone is encouraged to dig in and create his or her version of the perfect sundae. It can be as simple or elaborate as the individual envisions it. For an added twist, once the creations are finished, give your sundae to someone else to eat, so another at the table can share his or her reality with you. All the recipes are included at the end of this chapter.

The first step in preparing this Celebration Dinner is to

We call upon the Earth,
our planet home, with its
beautiful depths and
soaring heights,
its vitality and abundance
of life, and together we
ask that it teach us, and
show us the Way.
We call upon the land
which grows our food,
the nurturing soul, the
fertile fields,
the abundant gardens and
orchards, and ask that
they teach us, and show
us the Way.

— Chinook Blessing

assemble the necessary ingredients. With recipes in hand, take an inventory of your refrigerator and pantry to determine what you will need to harvest or purchase in order to make the dishes, while noting what you already have on hand. Make a grocery list, organized according to where you will need to shop for the items.

For the soup and main course, you will acquire your organic squash, onions, tomatoes, green beans, and fresh herbs at a greengrocer or an organic farm stand, and the oat milk, sunflower seeds, and almond butter for the soup at a natural foods store or well-stocked supermarket. You will want to buy the freshest organic ingredients you can find in order to benefit the most from the life force. As you select your fresh food, think of the higher purpose of all the ingredients and the process involved for bringing them to your table. Visualize the food in its natural environment, growing in the rich soil, bathed in the sun's rays, and absorbing the light that you will receive when you eat it.

Begin your meal preparation by washing and cutting the vegetables, recalling the rice-washing contemplation and the Seeing the Life Force exercise in chapter 1. Practicing your meditation routine before you begin can help set your mental stage and open your heart with love. At this time, offer a prayer or blessing to direct healing energy through your heart, head, and hands directly into the food. Don't be surprised if your awareness of it opens the energy channels within your body, and you begin to feel wonderful. Use a blessing such as this.

Father-Mother God,
Sanctify my heart and mind
As I prepare the life force for those I love.
May your vibrant healing energy
Pass through my hands
And into our food as I thank you
For your bountiful gifts.

Be mindful of the sacred alchemy of cooking. Your every breath is part of the total harmony as you cook this centered meal.

No longer a chore, even if you're tired and had a bad day, let this dinner receive your energy and the blessings of the Creator. As you do this, leave all other concerns outside the door, and you will be energized in the process. Close your eyes and breathe deeply as you prepare to honor and enhance the life force in the food. Just "be" with the cooking.

When cutting vegetables, notice the symmetries, colors, aromas, and textures. Actually feel the subtle energies of the foods. Continue this mindful reverence through each step of the preparation and cooking process, right on to the garnishing and serving of your meal.

Begin your Celebration Dinner with a prayer or benediction of thanks for the food and how it got there, for everyone at the table, and for life. As you eat your meal, remember to chew slowly and mindfully as you call your attention to the taste and texture of each bite.

If you practice this mindfulness every time you cook, the sacred kitchen will manifest beyond the space itself to become a healing force in your life and a positive contribution to the healing of the world. While the Celebration Dinner works beautifully as the featured meal in any tradition, it is especially well suited for a new tradition called the Feast of Light, a ritual intended to bring together the peoples of every nation and religious background for the purpose of tolerance, mutual respect, and global unity through love.

THE UNIVERSAL LOVE OF LIGHT

In chapter 5, we explored religious and social celebrations as well as some of the practices that spiritually link the peoples of the world. Some of those themes include celebrations of the New Year, the seasons, planting, harvest, commemorations of historical or religious events, and mandates from Scripture.

If you wished to choose a single theme that is most universally honored, regardless of belief system or nationality, and turn it into a new tradition, what could be better than celebrating light?

This is the message which we have heard of him and proclaim to you, that God is light and in him is no darkness at all.

— John 1:5

The theme of light is at home in every faith and philosophy, every tribe, community, and nation, and rightly so.

After creating the heavens and the earth, God's first act was to create light. Light is celebrated in many religions as the etheric light of consciousness, the infusion of the Holy Spirit, the divine sparks that we call the souls of humankind. Jesus told the people: "You are the light of the world," and "let your light so shine before men." Hanukkah is the eight-day Jewish celebration called the Festival of the Lights, commemorating the miracle of a day's worth of oil miraculously burning for eight days. Saint Lucia is the Queen of Light. The canon of every religion speaks of light.

Few religions formalize a festival dedicated to light. However, a Festival of Lights called Diwali is one of the most important of Hindu feasts. It takes place during the Hindu month of Kartika (October–November), the beginning of the Indian winter and the new year of their calendar. During Diwali, the goddess of prosperity, Lakshmi, visits every house that is lit to welcome her. So, households everywhere light little oil lamps, candles, or strings of electric lights. Like the Chinese New Year (Spring Festival), celebrants clean house, bathe, and dress in new clothes. They feast on a breakfast of *massoor dal*, orange-colored lentils, as orange in their culture symbolizes wealth and abundance.

Light perfectly symbolizes the life-giving attributes of the Creator, the debut of creation in the great eye of God, the ecstatic vibrating of the immortal soul, and the flame of consciousness itself. As we consider a new tradition to awaken the sacredness of the kitchen, we might wonder if it is acceptable to blend aspects from different belief systems. But spiritual traditions of the world host plenty of crossovers. There is beauty and unity in diversity, if within that diversity we can honor the great truths we hold in common. Therein lies the secret to keeping a sacred kitchen.

With this colorful global variety in mind, the authors propose the Feast of Light, a universal celebration that can dovetail into any belief system. Celebrate the universal light once a year with people of all faiths, the world over. Its purpose is to galvanize the oneness of the guests with each other, as well as with everyone who recognizes the gift of light around the globe.

The Feast of Light

As calendars and religious holidays vary, the Feast of Light should be planned for some recurring celestial event. It should favor neither a particular culture's calendar, religious tradition, nor even hemisphere. We chose September 22, the day the sun enters Libra each year, because Libra is the sign of the zodiac that depicts balance. The holiday would officially begin at sunrise by those who rise to greet the sun and would end at sunset with a ritual feast.

The ceremony is simple, and the few needed implements are accessible by stockbroker or villager alike: a white candle, a glass of wine (or grape juice), and the prayers and invocations provided below.

If you are up at dawn, begin the day with the Prayer for Light. Face east, whether alone or in a group. If with a group, join hands and form a circle.

Prayer for Light

I give thanks unto you O Lord,
For you have illumined my face
With the light of your covenant.
Day by day I seek you,
And ever you shine upon me
Bright as the perfect dawn.
— from the Qumran scrolls, *Book of Hymns*, IV, 5–V, 5

You can repeat the Prayer for Light at high noon, as a reminder during the day of the crucial function that light serves for us and for our world. Throughout the day, incorporate any other group prayer or meditation practices you may have. It would be consistent with many traditions to spend part of the day cleaning your house and setting out new clothes to wear during the Celebration Dinner. Kahlil Gibran wrote, "Work is love made visible," so the tasks shouldn't be thought of as chores, but works that honor the Creator and the light of the soul that lives in each of us. Let the main ritual of the feast be the Celebration Dinner.

First, light the candle and let it burn in a prominent place

Radiance alone is eternal.

— Pashupata-Brahmana-
Upanishad (II.21)

Let There Be Light!

Christianity: "Ye are the Light of the world." (Matthew 5:14)

Hinduism: "In the effulgent lotus of the heart dwells Brahman, the Light of lights." (Mundaka Upanishad)

Islam: "Allah is the Light of the heavens and the earth." (The Holy Qur'an, Sura 24:35)

Judaism: "The Lord is my Light; whom shall I fear?" (Psalm 27:1)

Buddhism: "The radiance of Buddha shines ceaselessly." (The Dhammapada)

Shinto: "The Light of Divine Amaterasu shines forever." (The Kurozumi Munetada)

Sikhism: "God, being Truth, is the one Light of all." (Adi Granth)

Taoism: "Following the Light, the sage takes care of all." (Lao Tzu)

Zoroastrianism: "First I have made the Kingdom of Light, dear to all Life." (The Zend Avesta)

while dinner is being prepared. Use a long one that will last through the celebration's end. As the candle is being lit, let everyone in attendance read The Blessing of the Bounty in unison, intoning together the OM: the sound of the Allness of God.

The Blessing of the Bounty

OM!

Beloved Mother Nature
You are here on our table as our food.
You are endlessly bountiful, benefactress of all.

Please grant us health and strength, wisdom and dispassion,
To find permanent Peace and Joy,
And to share this Peace and Joy with one and all.
Mother Nature is my mother,
My father is the Lord of All,
All the peoples are my relatives,
The entire universe is my home.
I offer this unto OM
That Truth which is Universal

May the entire universe be filled with Peace and Joy, Love
* and Light.*
May the light of Truth overcome all darkness! Victory to
* that Light!*

       — Sri Swami Satchidananda, the Anna Poorna

If time permits and family or guests are participating, begin the dinner by giving thanks and blessing the ingredients before preparing the food. Next, wash and cut the vegetables together. We use the prayer above at this step, although you can compose your own, just as couples now write their own wedding vows.

As the food is being prepared, those gathered can choose to talk and have fun or to make cooking an act of reverence, spending the time in the silent, moving meditation of preparation. If you choose the latter, remind everyone to keep their minds focused on the life force in the foods, on their origin from Father God, of their sustenance in Mother Earth, the priestly office of the cook, and sacred alchemy of cooking.

While dinner is cooking, everyone should dress in new clothes that were laid out before dinner, symbolizing new beginnings. Once dinner is placed on the table and the participants gathered, before being seated, stand for the benediction. Whether led by a leader or spoken in unison, read the benediction at the beginning of the meal. This focuses the thoughts of those present, and unifies hearts for the mindful purpose at hand.

Benediction of the Feast

We invoke the spirit of God, creator of all life and giver of all gifts. Fill us with the light that opened the eyes of the prophets and the saints; ignite within us the light of understanding, tolerance, and gratitude. Let this Feast of Light signify our devotion to the light of truth wherever it manifests, within our brothers and sisters and within ourselves. Bless this meal, with which we nourish ourselves with the light from the sun in mindfulness of the Source of all life.

You can fashion rituals for use throughout your meal, incorporating ideas that conform with your belief system or that have special meaning to you. You can make the rituals of the Feast of Light as simple or elaborate as you wish. We suggest that whenever you sit down to celebrate, set a place at the table for an angel, a saint, a prophet, or just the spirit of a virtue or ideal you would like to weave into your life. At some point during the meal, offer a toast with the wine to life, abundance, and the love of the Father-Mother God. Finally, at meal's end, let everyone join in the Prayer of Gratitude for the Light, which we created from a poem by Ralph Waldo Emerson. You can, of course, write or borrow another one that has some significant universal meaning to you.

Prayer of Gratitude for the Light

For each new morning with its light
Forest and shelter of the night,
For health and food, for love and friends,
For everything Thy goodness sends.

— Ralph Waldo Emerson

Let the Feast of Light become an annual celebration of what every world citizen has in common: light, in all its literal and symbolic meanings. Use the Celebration Dinner, or adapt it with specialties from your own sacred kitchen. Invite your neighborhood, family, or friends to gather for the Feast of Light. Try to initiate one in your town or county. Periodically use celebrations and rituals from around the world, if only to honor our sacred traditions: our brotherhood and sisterhood under the Fatherhood of the Lord of all, nourished by the Motherhood of Earth.

YOUR KITCHEN TEMPLE

Spiritually, many people swing somewhere between periodic religious obligations and a wishful urge to "do something" about their spiritual needs. It is often difficult to make time for this and all too easy to complain about the chores that crowd the precious hours of the day. This is why it makes sense to use your newly reorganized and consecrated sacred kitchen as a place for mind-fully touching the Divine when you cook.

People find spiritual comfort in regular visits to their church-es, synagogues, or mosques. But many only visit their chosen houses of God out of obligation or intimidation. It's a rare individ-ual who feels close to the Divine wherever he or she may go. Still, imagine being able to feel so unified with the Divine and so cen-tered throughout your day that you are always at peace with your-self and the world. It can be done, whatever your faith, but not without good mental habits and sincerity of motive.

Your success depends on your commitment to your spiritual ideals. But using the kitchen as a touchstone with the Divine can save your sanity in the day-to-day rat race. Where stress is con-cerned, it could even save your life.

"In violent and chaotic times such as these," writes author Sue Kaufman in her essay "Falling Bodies," in the anthology *Where the Heart Is,* "our only chance for survival lies in creating our own lit-tle islands of sanity and order, in making little havens of our homes." This is supported by the predictions of marketing fore-caster Faith Popcorn, who in her book *The Popcorn Report,* cor-rectly predicted the trend of "cocooning," in which people are sticking closer to home for protection, safety, or because they've become too busy and tired to go anywhere.

What better touchstone could there be than your kitchen tem-ple? It is now a place of prayer, rituals, and miracles, so let the kitchen, where you have to spend time anyway, be like a temple within your home. You don't need to physically turn your kitchen into a temple, but with the added touches from chapter 2, and your new attitude of reverence and conscientiously applied prayer, try to think of it as a temple whenever you enter.

After all, in many areas of the world, people designate some special place for worship in their homes. Buddhist homes, for example, feature a picture or statue of Buddha in a prominent place, and regularly burn incense — joss sticks — before it. Tibetan homes traditionally have three levels. The storeroom and stable occupy the ground level, the living area and kitchen are on the middle floor, and on the third is a prayer room, altar, and guest

The sun shall be no more
your light by day,
Nor for brightness shall
the moon give light to
you by night;
But the Lord will be your
everlasting light,
And your God will be
your glory.

— Isaiah 60:19

...Devote all time and resources at your disposal to the building up of a fine kitchen. It will be, as it should be, the most comforting and comfortable room in the house.

— Elizabeth David

room. This sense of the sacred in the home is lacking in the West.

You could do worse than establish such a place for worship in your home. But in a sacred kitchen, busy Westerners can catch up on their spiritual work while they do their kitchen work. It's all in our attitude, mindfulness, and intent, from harvesting the vegetables or buying the groceries to putting dinner on the table.

Even if your kitchen is little more than a stove and sink in a tiny studio apartment, you can add those touches that will remind you that you have designated this space as sacred in your home. As mentioned in chapter 2, you can create a holy atmosphere by placing a meaningful religious symbol on the wall or doorframe, or a piece of statuary or stained-glass art in front of the window — anything that will be visible as you enter or approach the kitchen. Let your activity there be like that of a monk or priestess. Every time you enter, anticipate a peaceful, sacred kitchen. Enter your kitchen with reverence. After all, you are very important: You keep everyone you feed alive!

In the pages of this book, we have encouraged you to create a new relationship with your cooking space. As with a person, let this relationship open your eyes to new possibilities. Look forward to being in your kitchen. Anticipate the healing moments that you will spend there and your closeness to the life force in the foods. Think of the alchemy you perform, turning the Creator's life-giving gifts into a meal that will not only please the eye, the nose, and the palate, but that will sustain life itself for you and anyone fortunate enough to dine with you.

Remember to carry forward into every area of your life the peace of that sweet creamy center of yourself that you contact in meditation. Approach everything you do with mindfulness, wherever you work, leaving all other problems and concerns outside the kitchen door. Rise above the stresses with your centered mind and a body fresh and healthy from your centered-cuisine diet. Let all chores and housework become "love made visible," and let no labor be wasted by neglecting to dedicate it to manifesting God's love on earth.

In a sacred kitchen, higher-consciousness cooking becomes a

stress-free meditation by which you clear your mind and restore your connection to the Divine. It is the sacred temple in which your holy alchemy becomes a nourishing flame of beauty in your home and community. It extends your reach beyond the body to the souls of those you feed. It bestows a blessing on your guests that extends to all those they meet long after they leave your table. Ultimately, the miracles you create in your sacred kitchen can help to create a future on earth in which all the peoples of the world will thrive with abundance and health.

There are places in which fields burst with fresh food, and places elsewhere in which drought, famine, and war keep whole populations in a state of perpetual starvation. Kitchen power is universal and part of the perpetual-motion machine of the World Mother. It is up to us all to keep the global kitchen open around the clock. We must reach out across the miles and the boundaries with our long spoons to feed our brothers and sisters. Within our own homes, we must reach out to each other with the Creator's abundance, rich with the life force out of the generous cook pot of the Divine Mother.

With your higher-consciousness ideas, just try now to avoid thinking about the miracles you perform while you are in your kitchen! You have become connected to the global kitchen by mindfully cooking with purpose, and by turning every meal into a form of worship of the Creator through simple rituals and deliberate celebration. May your cooking now have a positive spiritual effect on your household and on the planet. May the temple of your sacred kitchen be forevermore a source of leavening in your spiritual life.

RECIPES FOR A CELEBRATION DINNER

The following recipes were chosen for the Celebration Dinner because each of them expresses major elements found in *The Sacred Kitchen*. Our first course, Potage du Soleil, uses fresh summer squash and is combined with rich almond butter and oat milk for a sublime soup that exemplifies creamy richness without dairy products. Both the Celebration Salmagundi and Eight-Treasure

The Prayer of St. Francis of Assisi

Lord, make me an instrument of thy peace.
Where there is hatred, let me sow love;
Where there is injury, pardon;
Where there is doubt, faith;
Where there is despair, hope;
Where there is darkness, light;
Where there is sadness, joy.
Oh Divine Master,
Grant that I may not so much
Seek to be consoled as to console,
To be understood as to understand,
To be loved as to love;
For it is in giving that we receive,
It is in pardoning that we are pardoned,
And it is in dying that we are born to eternal life.

Rice are dishes that combine many diverse ingredients to form a whole, thus symbolizing the global community. They also use many fresh vegetables that are rich in chi. The Create-Your-Own-Reality Sundaes dessert is a hands-on way to express creativity and sharing, and to engender fun and playfulness in a family meal.

POTAGE DU SOLEIL

This "soup of the sun" can brighten any meal. The oat milk is rich in nutrients and has the perfect flavor and texture for use in cream soups. It is available in natural foods stores as is the almond butter.

1 tablespoon canola oil
1 large onion, sliced
6 yellow summer squash, chopped
3 cups Vital Vegetable Stock (page 172)

1 1/2 cups oat milk
1 tablespoon almond butter
Salt and freshly ground pepper to taste
2 tablespoons sunflower seeds for garnish

Heat the oil in a large saucepan over medium heat. Add the onions, cover, and cook for 5 minutes. Add the squash and stock and simmer, uncovered, for 15 minutes, or until the vegetables are soft. Puree the mixture in a blender or food processor until smooth, working in batches if necessary. Add the oat milk, almond butter, salt, and pepper. To serve cold, transfer the soup to a container and refrigerate for several hours. To serve hot, return the soup to the saucepan and reheat gently, being careful not to boil. Garnish with sunflower seeds.

Serves 4

CELEBRATION SALMAGUNDI

Vary the vegetables in this delicious concoction according to seasonal availability and personal taste. Meaty chunks of seitan, tempeh, or firm tofu may be substituted for the beans.

1 tablespoon canola oil
1 large onion, chopped
4 carrots, cut into 1/2-inch dice
1 large garlic clove, minced
1 pound tomatoes, peeled and chopped
3 cups water
1 bay leaf
1/2 teaspoon minced fresh thyme, or 1/4 teaspoon
    dried thyme
Salt and freshly ground pepper to taste
8 ounces green beans, trimmed and cut into 1-inch

For the Lord your God is bringing you into a good land, a land of brooks of water, of fountains and springs, flowing forth in valleys and hills, a land of wheat and barley, of vines and fig trees and pomegranates, a land of olive trees and honey, a land in which you will eat bread without scarcity, in which you will lack nothing, a land whose stones are iron, and out of whose hills you can dig copper. And you shall eat and be full, and you shall bless the Lord your God for the good land he has given you.

— Deuteronomy 8:7–11

pieces
1 cup fresh or frozen peas
2 cups cooked Great Northern beans
Eight-Treasure Rice (recipe follows)

Heat the oil in a large saucepan over medium heat. Add the onion and carrots and sauté for 5 minutes. Add the garlic and sauté for 30 seconds. Add the tomatoes and sauté for 1 minute. Add the water, bay leaf, thyme, salt, and pepper. Bring to a boil, reduce heat to a simmer, cover, and cook for 20 minutes. Discard the bay leaf. Add the green beans and simmer the stew for 15 minutes. Add the peas and Great Northern beans and simmer for 15 minutes if using fresh peas or 5 minutes if using frozen, or until the green beans and peas are tender. Divide the rice among 4 large plates and top with the salmagundi.

Serves 4

EIGHT-TREASURE RICE

Studded with jewel-toned vegetable treasures, this rice can be a meal in itself, but it adds a colorful touch to the meal when used as a bed for salmagundi. This recipe needs to use cold cooked rice for best results. Use the Brown Rice with Love (page 21).

3 tablespoons tamari sauce
1 tablespoon toasted sesame oil
$1/8$ teaspoon cayenne pepper
1 tablespoon canola oil
1 small red bell pepper, seeded, deribbed, and finely chopped
1 cup finely shredded cabbage
1 carrot, finely grated
$1/4$ cup minced scallion
1 garlic clove, minced

1 teaspoon minced fresh ginger
3 cups cold cooked rice
2 tablespoons sesame seeds
2 tablespoons minced fresh parsley

Combine the tamari, sesame oil, and cayenne in a shallow bowl. Heat the canola oil in a large skillet over medium heat. Add the bell pepper, cabbage, carrot, and scallion and stir-fry for 2 minutes. Add the garlic and ginger and stir-fry until fragrant, about 30 seconds. Stir in the tamari mixture. Add the rice and stir-fry until heated through and well combined about 5 minutes. Serve garnished with sesame seeds and parsley.

Serves 4

CREATE-YOUR-OWN-REALITY SUNDAES

Invite family and friends to gather around a table laden with sundae makings, from a variety of dessert glasses and bowls, to a selection of sorbets, frozen yogurt, and nondairy frozen desserts. Ask everyone to think about what would make the perfect sundae, and then to create it. Let everyone assemble his or her own sundae, then give it to the person opposite to eat. Thus everyone involved participates in creating and sharing his or her own reality with another.

2 or 3 pints non-dairy frozen dessert, sorbet, or frozen yogurt (choice of flavors)

FOR THE TOPPINGS:
Fresh berries, sliced fruit or cooked fruit toppings
Ground nuts
Chocolate sauce
Whipped cream or tofu whipped cream

For this final course of the Celebration Dinner, clear the table of the previous course and then arrange the dessert components on the table. For convenience, you may pre-scoop the frozen dessert, sorbet, or frozen yogurt by softening it slightly several hours before serving time and scooping it onto a baking sheet. Let the scoops reharden in the freezer, then when ready to serve, transfer the scoops to a serving plate or bowl. Arrange the berries, fruit, or toppings on a platter or in bowls. Use smaller bowls to hold the nuts, chocolate, and other toppings. Place a selection of serving bowls and spoons on the table and explain the symbolism of the dessert to everyone at the table. Then, dig in and enjoy. Refrigerate and/or freeze any leftovers for another use.

Serves 4 to 6

An Ancient Hindu Blessing

This ritual is One
The food is One
We who offer the food are One
The fire of hunger is also One
All action is One
We who understand this are One.

7

Recipes for a
Sacred Kitchen

*The art of cooking, of using fire, water, and salt, is the art of
alchemy in the kitchen. . . . Through the art of cooking, man has
learned how to adapt to his environment, to the changing seasons,
and to his changing needs, physically, mentally, and spiritually.
This is the key to humankind's ultimate freedom.*

— Cecile Tovah Levin, *Cooking for Regeneration*

This chapter features a collection of centered recipes developed by Robin
Robertson to support the principles of *The Sacred Kitchen*. They are made
with fresh, healthful ingredients and can be mixed and matched to create complete vegetarian meals. They have been designed to be esthetically appealing,
nutritionally sound, low in fat, and with all the flavor of the classic cuisines. The
chapter also contains sections on ingredients, menu planning, and suggestions
for keeping a food journal, all geared to make cooking in your sacred kitchen a
rewarding experience. The chapter is followed by a resources directory.

COOKING IN A SACRED KITCHEN

By now you know what a sacred kitchen is and may have taken steps to create one in your home. You may have already tried some of the recipes in the previous chapters. Perhaps this book has helped you begin to feel your connection to the Divine while you cook. Hopefully, you are tuning into the life force and beginning to cook with love in your new peaceful, stress-free environment. In that space, you are naturally more open to your inner inspiration, guidance, and creativity. Here is how to apply it in your kitchen.

Imagine yourself as an artist when you cook. Think of a recipe not as a rigid rule, but as your guide, your "subject," your model. Read a recipe first for comprehension and then a second time to assemble the ingredients, making sure you have everything you need. (If you're missing an ingredient, this is an opportunity to make a creative substitution. You may already be doing this with familiar family recipes that you know by heart.)

Next, realize that preparing and seasoning food is a personal matter. Subtle nuances, varied seasonings, alternative ingredients all combine to make one soup, stew, or stir-fry different from the next. Keep this in mind as you try these and other recipes.

As you gradually replace processed foods in your diet with fresh, natural ingredients, you may begin to realize that the ingredients themselves can provide the "flavors" of the meal. A dash of sea salt or a splash of tamari sauce, for example, may be all that is needed to bring out the flavor in a particular dish.

The use of varied seasonings is a treasured secret to maintaining a full repertoire of international cuisines. Along with an array of fresh herbs, judicious use of spices such as cayenne, cumin, and curry powder will help ensure that you won't have to worry about serving "boring" food. Spice up your meals with chili paste, salsa, or maybe a hot Thai or Szechuan sauce. And, of course, you will want tomatoes, garlic, and cooking wines to find their way into your saucepan to create just the right flavor in many dishes.

Therein lies the epicurean consciousness of the centered cuisine described in chapter 4. It's an awareness of the herbs and spices, of seasonings, and of regional flavors that add variety and interest to foods. It is also a discriminating sense of the classic culinary traditions tempered by what's fashionable in the ever-changing "what's hot what's not" food trend cycles. Use this awareness to be creative with the preferences of family and friends, the universal desire for comfort foods, and all your old family recipes. These combined elements become the fabric of a centered cuisine when sewn together with the sturdy thread of healthful, balanced ingredients.

Following is some basic information on centered grains, beans, vegetables, soups, condiments, and desserts that can help you showcase a centered cuisine in your sacred kitchen.

GRAINS

If you have ever eaten a bowl of plain, unadorned rice, you may be wondering how a grain-based diet can be made interesting. The fact is, the variety of grains and products now being made from them is surpassed only by the number of delicious ways in which you can prepare them. Grains can be used as a wholesome bed on which to nestle delicious concoctions of vegetables, beans, and sauces. Grains can also be used in everything from soups to stuffings and desserts. Wheat can even be made into a roast (see Thankful Holiday Roast recipe on page 88). Brown, or whole-grain, rice is the most centered of the grains. It's versatile and easily obtained, so it makes an ideal everyday grain. The familiar starchy white rice we grew up on is actually brown rice that has been stripped of many of its important nutrients — all that remains is the starchy white center. Eating it does little more than fill you up — and out. Then, it creates in your body a craving for more food because the nutrition just wasn't there. Brown rice is rice the way nature grows it, and therefore, the most beneficial form. Brown rice grows in three different grain sizes — short, medium, and long — and is the preferred rice specified for many of the recipes in this book.

Other grains include corn, wheat, barley, oats, teff, millet, spelt, quinoa, amaranth, kamut, and couscous (actually a milled

I do this chore
not just to get it
out of the way,
but as the way
to make real
kind connected mind.

May I awaken to what
these ingredients offer,
and may I awaken
best I can
energy, warmth,
imagination,
this offering of heart
and hand.

— Edward Espe Brown,
The Tassajara Recipe Book

wheat product). Each grain has its own character and history, as well as nutritional value and a unique flavor that can lend a global flair to your meals.

Whole-grain pastas, such as soba, made from buckwheat, and udon, made from whole wheat, add an interesting dimension to your grain options. Breads provide another easy and delectable way to ensure that you are getting enough grain each day. There is a wide range of whole-grain breads available in most natural foods stores, each with distinct textures and flavors.

The most unique member of the grain family is seitan. Also called "wheat meat," because it is made from wheat, seitan is chewy and can be very meatlike in appearance and texture. Seitan is made from wheat gluten, the part of wheat flour that remains after the starch and bran are eliminated. Gluten is made through a simple process of kneading flour dough and rinsing it several times. It is high in protein, calcium, and niacin, and freezes well. Seitan can be made from scratch, although a "quick-mix" seitan product is available from Arrowhead Mills for those times when there's no time for kneading. Precooked seitan is also available in the refrigerated section of most natural food stores and many supermarkets. It is usually found in the form of meaty chunks, ready to use in recipes. The recipes in this book calling for seitan will specify precooked, or quick-mix, seitan.

BEANS

Beans have been grown and eaten in cultures all over the world since ancient times. They are traditionally combined with grains in almost all corners of the globe, from India to Mexico to the Middle East. No matter how you prepare them, beans are a natural complement to whole grains, and as you plan your whole-grain meals, you should try to include a place for beans at your table.

The small red adzuki bean is a great bean for everyday use. Adzuki beans are very high in protein and, after being soaked overnight, cook in an hour. This makes them ideal for cooking right along with your rice. By cooking brown rice and adzuki beans together, you are combining two wonderful sources of protein. The addition of some steamed or stir-fried vegetables is all it takes for a complete, well-balanced meal.

Other quick-cooking beans include split peas and lentils, neither of which requires soaking. They make great hearty soups, and lentils are also delicious when used in various pasta dishes and spreads.

Longer-cooking beans include black beans, Great Northerns, kidneys, limas, navy beans, pintos, and chickpeas. These all require overnight soaking and can take up to two or three hours to cook. For convenience, these longer-cooking beans can be cooked in large quantities and frozen in usable portions.

The most useful, versatile bean of all is the soybean. For years, soybeans have been hailed as one of humanity's greatest nutritional treasures since there are a number of high-protein foods that are derived from them, such as tofu, tempeh, okara, miso, and tamari and other sauces.

In recent years, tofu has grown in popularity to the point where it is now readily available in most supermarkets. Tofu is a supple white curd, made during a process in which soybeans are cooked, ground, and then strained. The freshly strained soy "milk" is then curdled with a natural coagulant found in sea salt called *nigari*.

Easy to digest, tofu is high in protein, low in fat, and contains no cholesterol. It comes in various forms such as soft, medium, firm, and extra-firm. The firmer styles are used in lasagna, "eggless" egg salad, stir-fries, and for marinated and pan-fried dishes. This is because it holds together well and can stand up to handling. Regular tofu is sometimes called "Chinese" tofu. "Silken," or Japanese-style, is best for blending, mashing, or puréeing into creamy sauces, dressings, dips and cheesecakes, because they can be easily blended into a smooth, pourable texture. Regular soft tofu is packed in water whereas the silken varieties are usually found in asceptic containers.

Unfortunately, many people still turn up their noses at tofu, pronouncing it bland and flavorless. In fact, it is the very blandness of tofu that is its best feature. This protein- and calcium-rich

If we eat wrongly, no doctor can cure us; if we eat rightly, no doctor is needed.

— Dr. Victor G. Rocine, in 1930

food lends itself to all sorts of sauces, marinades, and seasonings. It can be transformed into anything, from a soup to a sauce to an entrée or dessert. And if it's cooked and seasoned properly, it is definitely not tasteless.

Other soybean products include tempeh and okara, two versatile meat alternatives. Tempeh is made by fermenting soybeans and pressing them into cakes, which can be grilled, sautéed, or stir-fried. Okara is made from the part of the soybean that remains after the tofu-making process. Rarely found on its own, okara is used as an ingredient in vegetarian burgers and cutlets. In addition to these soy "meats," other products, such as soy milk, soy cheese, miso, and tamari and other soy sauces, also come from the versatile soybean. Tamari sauce and miso are soy products that are indispensable in centered cuisine. Be sure to look for a good tamari soy sauce that has no additives or preservatives, unlike most regular soy sauces. One look at the ingredients on the soy sauce label will tell you why. Most contain corn syrup, artificial coloring, and other additives, whereas a good tamari sauce will be unadulterated. Flavorful "low-sodium" and "wheat-free" tamari sauces are also available.

Miso, a fermented soybean paste, makes a nutritious soup as well as an enrichment for sauces and dressings. Available in different colors and degrees of saltiness, miso is high in protein and rich in enzymes that aid digestion. Miso paste also makes a good base for sauces, gravies, stews, and salad dressings.

VEGETABLES

As you plan your dinner with grain-based entrées, consider your choices of vegetables: green, yellow, white, or red. This is the color spectrum of vegetables, all full of life, free of chemicals, fresh and pure.

No longer relegated to the lowly position of side dish, vegetables are finally coming into their own in today's new cooking trends. Since vegetables are an important part of your daily food intake in a centered diet, it is helpful to know how to prepare a large variety of vegetables in a number of ways, such as steaming, sautéing, grilling, and baking. Each day should include some green vegetables, such as broccoli or kale; some "ground" vegetables, such as butternut or acorn squash; and some root vegetables, like carrots and onions. By including vegetables from the various categories, you are ensuring a well-rounded nutritional intake. Whenever possible, try to select organic produce for optimum flavor and nutrition. Vegetables should be thoroughly washed or scrubbed before using, and peeled when appropriate, especially if not organic.

Vegetables add much to the esthetics of a meal as well. An eye for symmetry and balance in color, shape, and proportion of the food you present is an important factor. Beauty has a strong psychological effect on the person eating the food.

While fresh vegetables are best, there are a few special helpers that should be kept on hand in the cupboard and freezer. Keep a bag of green peas in the freezer for tossing a handful into a grain pilaf, pasta salad, or a casserole. Frozen peas come in handy when you need an extra dimension of color and flavor, and they can be added to a dish in the frozen state — they will defrost and heat through by the time the rest of the dish is ready. When using frozen peas in a pasta salad or other cold dish, just run the peas under hot water to defrost them.

Other handy menu transformers to keep in the cupboard are artichoke hearts, pimientos, capers, olives, sun-dried tomatoes, sauerkraut, water chestnuts, and dried shiitake mushrooms. These flavorful "secret" ingredients can greatly increase your mealtime options.

SOUPS

Part of the concept of a centered cuisine is to balance, not only the food you eat, but the ways in which the food is prepared. It is a good idea to enjoy your foods prepared in a variety of ways — to keep yourself from getting stuck in the rut of eating the "same old thing."

When you're in a hurry, nothing beats a bowl of soup combined with a sandwich or a salad, or both. They are easy to

If you can organize your
kitchen, you can organize
your life.

— Louis Parrish

prepare, and at the same time, nourishing and delicious. This popular mealtime combination can provide an especially good opportunity to enjoy a wide variety of vegetarian choices, and introduce meat-free meals to your family.

Soup is a great way to get a concentrated amount of nutrition in one serving. It is economical and easy to make, keeps well, is easy to reheat, freezes well, and is filling without being fattening. Whether a soup is served to herald the coming of the rest of the meal, or to shine as the star of the meal itself, it should complement the rest of the meal in its taste, texture, and appeal. Soups can be categorized as clear soups, cream soups or bisques, and hearty soups or chowders. If you are serving a rich, hearty meal, serve a light, clear-broth soup. Conversely, if your meal is light, a thick, hearty soup is in order.

The next time someone in your home catches a cold, why not replace "Mom's chicken soup" with a rich bowl of miso soup (with all its immune-system strengthening properties), brimming with chunks of tofu, slivers of vegetables, and a savory broth? Who's to say it's the chicken in chicken soup that made "Mom's penicillin" the universal cure-all? Maybe it was the reaction in the body to the hot liquid and high concentration of vegetable nutrients. Perhaps this was combined with the fact that Mom prepared her special soup with a mother's love and concern that it would make you well. A hearty vegetable soup made with love and miso may well become the "chicken soup" cure of the next generation.

The basis of a good soup is a good stock. A rich vegetable stock may be achieved by simply saving all your cooking liquids when you prepare vegetables and combining them. You can then add vegetable trimmings from such vegetables as onions, carrots, parsley, celery, cabbage, and squash. Simmer the mixture for a delicious stock that can be used as the basis for any soup, as well as sauces and gravies. For added taste and nutrition, stock can also be used to replace the water in most recipes, such as when cooking grains. Stock can be made ahead and portioned and frozen for future use.

CONDIMENTS AND SEASONINGS

Condiments and seasonings are to a meal as the final brush strokes are to an oil painting: They bring it to life and make it complete. The way food is seasoned can mean the difference between a dish that is bland and boring, and one that is delicious. It's all in the "brush stroke" of inspired use of seasonings and condiments.

Some popular condiments used to enliven meals include fresh ginger, mustards, chutneys, salsas, horseradish, chili paste, and infused oils and vinegars. There are also prepared sauces to keep on hand, such as teriyaki, hoisin, and a basic barbecue sauce that can add magic to a meal.

SWEET ALTERNATIVES

Grain sweeteners, such as barley malt and brown rice syrup, and natural fruit sweeteners are delicious and highly recommended. There is no "sugar rush" from rice syrup and barley malt because they are made from grain and metabolize more slowly in the system. In this context, since honey is not grain-based and metabolizes more quickly, it is not the most "centered" sweetener, although it is still a far better choice than refined sugar.

Try a natural dessert such as an apple pie made with brown rice syrup that allows for the natural sweetness of the fruit to come through, and you'll become a believer. Another sweetener that is preferable to sugar is Sucanat which is naturally derived dehydrated sugar cane juice.

If you're an ice-cream-aholic, you'll be happy to know that there are also several nondairy frozen desserts in your natural foods store freezer case, including Tofutti and Rice Dream, both of which come in many delicious flavors in addition to individual bars coated with carob and nuts. These products are so creamy, you'll find yourself marveling at the fact that they contain no dairy.

If you truly want to center yourself through diet, physically, mentally, and emotionally, the best thing you can do is to eliminate meat and sugar. This will break the vicious cycle of cravings. By substituting more moderate, centering foods, such as whole grains

I find the ritual of sharing meals with friends or family — especially wholesome natural foods — nourishes the spirit as well as the body.

— Mary Estella,
Natural Foods Cookbook

and vegetables, your body will find its balance. But as our dessert recipes illustrate, centered cuisine is not about deprivation. It is about life and living, and the enjoyment of earth's bounty. Most traditional dessert recipes are readily adaptable by substituting a grain-based sweetener for sugar, and an egg replacer, tofu, soy milk, or nut milk for dairy. Try some of your own favorite dessert recipes and substitute these ingredients. You may need to adjust the proportions, more or less, but experimenting is half the fun, because you get to eat your mistakes.

KITCHEN STRATEGIES

From time-saving tips to choosing cookware, there are a number of kitchen strategies to help you organize your time and take steps toward managing your mealtime routines.

Time-Saving Tips

Just because you have a sacred kitchen doesn't mean you have to spend all day there! There are some tried-and-true kitchen timesavers that can be incorporated into your kitchen routine to make the best use of your time in the kitchen.

An important part of feeling relaxed and well organized in your kitchen is to plan your menus in advance. That way you won't be panicked at dinnertime because of not knowing where to begin. You can start by simply planning the day before for the next evening's dinner, or plan an entire week's worth of menus at a time, which can help cut down on extra trips to the supermarket.

Keep a well-stocked freezer and refrigerator. This will allow you ample choices (presumably from your planned menus) with ingredients at your fingertips. Keeping a full larder also helps when a creative urge to cook up something strikes at the spur of the moment, or for unexpected company.

Planned leftovers can be a great time-saving strategy. When making dinner, remember to ask yourself if there's a second meal possibility there. For example, plan to make a chili casserole from last night's chili; transform leftover stew into a potpie; thicken leftover vegetable soup for a creamy pasta primavera sauce. Another strategy is to simply add a new sauce to give a basic dish new life: leftover stir-fried vegetables and rice take on a new personality when a curry sauce is added!

Here are some other handy hints:

- Buy grains and dried beans in bulk to save time and money and avoid wasteful packaging.
- Keep an arsenal of exciting sauces on hand to dress up simple meals in a flash: Salsa, chili paste, hoisin sauce, teriyaki sauce, curry paste, chutney, and jerk sauce can be miracle workers.
- Double your pleasure: Cook double batches of longer-cooking dishes that improve with age (such as stews and chili) to serve again later in the week.
- Freeze portions of longer-cooking ingredients such as beans and grains. Although fresh is best, sometimes fresh-frozen can be better in a pinch than resorting to canned, processed or worse — junk food — because "there's nothing to eat."

Shopping Strategies

The best advice when grocery shopping is to read labels. Even if you are shopping at a natural foods store, it is a good idea to read ingredients labels to make sure that you are buying products of the highest nutritional value. At the same time, careful shopping can produce the lowest negative impact on the environment of your home and the ecology of the planet.

Another example of careful shopping is to buy organic. Buy from a local organic farmer if possible, as his or her farming methods produce the highest-quality food without polluting the land, water, or air. Your purchases will help support your local organic agrarian economy.

It is also important, as much as possible, to buy seasonal foods. Foods grown out of season are artificially coaxed into existence through lighting or chemicals. In addition, foods from developing nations may not be chemically free, as laws differ throughout the world.

Choosing Cookware

Choosing the proper cookware is an important part of cooking in a sacred kitchen. You'll want to base your choice on what materials are best to promote good health and positive energy flow.

Some people avoid aluminum cookware because of its uneven heat distribution and tendency to scratch easily. Nonstick cookware has a tendency to chip, thus allowing impurities to mix with the food. The following are the best choices:

- **Stainless steel** is a popular choice because it provides good, even heat distribution, is easy to clean, and does not add toxic elements to food.
- **Glass** is a good choice because it doesn't interact with food and conveniently goes from stove top to refrigerator to freezer.
- **Ceramic cookware, or porcelain-covered cast iron**, has the double advantage of the non-porous cooking surface of porcelain and the even heat distribution of cast iron.
- **Cast iron** is a good choice for those who need to add extra iron to their diet. The down side is that it is heavy to use and needs extra care to maintain.

MENU PLANNING

Planning your meals a week in advance makes creating your grocery list easier and also helps you organize your time. Menu planning is also a good tool for keeping your meals varied and interesting. It can serve as a cross check to ensure that you are eating a well-balanced diet. While natural whole foods prepared fresh daily is our ideal, it is often unrealistic, given people's busy schedules and the time it take to prepare certain dishes, such as long-cooking grains, beans, sauces, and stews. As mentioned in the time-saving tips above, a compromise solution is to make large batches of your favorite long-cooking dishes and freeze portions for use later in the week. Frozen homemade food is the next best thing to fresh, since, unlike the frozen entrées you buy in supermarkets, it is unprocessed and wholesome.

Start your week by cooking large quantities of brown rice, spaghetti sauce, and a rich stew. With organization, you can accomplish this in two hours. Choose a day when you have time to spend at least two hours in the kitchen. Getting the whole family involved in this once-per-week exercise can help us get back to our Gaia roots — to the days every family member played a role vital to the survival of the family.

Once these dishes, or others of your choice, have been cooked and cooled to room temperature, portion them in containers and place the ones you will be serving soon in the refrigerator, and the rest in the freezer. The portions kept in the freezer can be removed, one container at a time as needed, becoming the basic ingredients for your own centered "fast food."

Now, let's take a look at a typical week, filling in all these entrées with seasonal vegetables, condiments, etc.

A Sample Week of Dinners

Use the following schedule as a guide for your own planning, using your favorite dishes. In this example, dinners revolve around three of the recipes in this book, Brown Rice with Love (page 21), Fresh Tomato Sauce (page 93), and Celebration Salmugundi, a vegetable stew (page 153). Add appetizers, desserts, and condiments as you desire.

Day 1: Brown rice topped with vegetable stew, served with warm, crusty bread.

Day 2: Whole-grain pasta with tomato sauce, served with salad.

Day 3: Stir-fried fresh vegetables with tofu, seasoned with a zesty sauce such as a Szechuan, curry, or Caribbean jerk sauce, served over brown rice.

Day 4. Vegetable stew used as the filling for a rich potpie or shepherd's pie.

> Give us this day our daily taste. Restore to us soups that spoons will not sink in and sauces which are never the same twice. Raise up among us stews with more gravy than we have bread to blot it with. Give us pasta with a hundred fillings.
>
> — Robert Farrar Capon, food writer

Day 5: Tomato sauce used to make a quick homemade pizza, topped with fresh vegetables and served with a salad.

Day 6: Stuffed winter squash filled with a savory stuffing made from the remaining brown rice with finely chopped sautéed vegetables, cloaked with a rich brown sauce (such as Magic Mushroom Sauce, page 193).

Day 7: Tofu lasagna, made with the remaining tomato sauce, served with salad.

With planning, preparing some of the elements for the following week's meals is really quite simple. All the meals above revolve around three initial dishes made at the beginning of the week. This example shows how you can simplify your cooking and still maintain enough variety to keep it interesting. If even more variety is desired, you can fill in with other recipes of your choice.

The recipes at the ends of chapters 1 through 6 provide delicious, well-balanced meals that are relevant to the material in those chapters. The following recipes are in keeping with the same spirit and can be used to create additional interesting menus, whether used individually or combined with other recipes.

Ideally, breakfasts should be nutritious, simple to prepare, and enjoyable. Many of us already eat a healthful breakfast of a whole-grain bread or cereal. This could be a bagel, a bowl of oatmeal, or a fruit smoothie. However, if you're used to eating scrambled eggs and sausage, the good news is that you can still enjoy a similar meal, using alternative ingredients. For example, make scrambled tofu with a pinch of turmeric for color and some chopped onions and other vegetables for flavor. Have some vegetarian sausage. Decide today to only eat whole-grain toast. You don't have to feel deprived to enjoy good-quality food. Instead, you should feel relieved to be ridding yourself of all that cholesterol, animal fat, and chemicals.

It is important to keep things in perspective. In a sacred kitchen, the goal is to cook with fresh, whole foods prepared fresh daily and in perfect balance for maximum nutrition.

Begin by familiarizing yourself with the new ingredients and bringing them into your home a few at a time. Start by introducing new side dishes to your table, and by making substitutions for meat and dairy in familiar recipes. You can adjust the time for each step to your particular needs, but it's best to be patient, both with yourself and your family. This gentle approach should take any "sting" out of making the transition.

KEEPING A JOURNAL

If making dietary changes involves a major transition for you, it may help you to keep a food journal. Use it to work up menu plans, note comments about new foods, and record how you're feeling about the new dietary changes. This is a good place to keep your recipes in order, especially any new recipes that you have created from old favorites, and other recipes that you find from various sources.

Included in your journal, you may want to keep a general list, by category, of all the healthful foods you want to add to your diet. This will help you decide where and how to introduce them, and also provide an at-a-glance overview of all the available possibilities.

ABOUT THE RECIPES IN THIS BOOK

The recipes in this book comprise a sampling of quick and easy ways to prepare delicious meals using healthful ingredients. The recipes provided in this chapter are organized in the following categories: soups, entrées, sides, sauces and dressings, desserts, and beverages. As discussed throughout the book, they are designed to give you a basic foundation of exciting new meal options that are simple to prepare and delightful to eat.

Centered cuisine presents a challenge to the adventurous cook. It asks you to prepare your favorite meat and dairy recipes without using meat or dairy, and still produce a delicious finished product. Once you've succeeded in navigating these uncharted waters, you'll feel like Magellan or Columbus with your newly discovered creation.

> Vegetables, as well as all foods, should be handled and treated with the greatest respect. They are the synthesis of the forces of Heaven and Earth giving themselves to us so that we can live. They are closer to us than our family and friends, actually transforming themselves into our very body and healing us of our sickness. This process Is a miracle of miracles and borders on the sacred.
>
> — Cecile Tovah Levin, *Cooking for Regeneration*

Centered cuisine goes beyond a set of prescribed recipes, extending itself into every culture and cuisine on earth, not just in these pages. For in truth, the recipes for a centered cuisine can be found not only in this book, but in Aunt Mary's recipe box, the Sunday newspaper, and the pages of magazines. With enough imagination and determination, a centered cuisine can be produced from old family recipes and general cookbooks as well, if you take what you've learned in these pages and look at your old recipes with new eyes.

RECIPES FOR A CENTERED CUISINE

SOUPS

VITAL VEGETABLE STOCK

A good vegetable stock is vital not only because it provides the basis for many recipes, but also because it's filled with the vital energy and nutrients of many healthful vegetables. This is a perfect recipe to start with if you want to learn to cook with intuition. Free yourself by reading through the recipe once for basic content, and then don't measure or time anything. Season, add or delete ingredients, and cook your stock using your intuition. Add more or less of any of the ingredients, and cook them as long as you think they need to cook. Taste and adjust the seasoning according to your own taste.

1 large onion, quartered
2 carrots, coarsely chopped
2 potatoes, diced
1 celery stalk, (including leaves) coarsely chopped
2 garlic cloves, crushed
1/2 cup coarsely chopped fresh parsley (including stems)
1 bay leaf

1 teaspoon salt
$1/_4$ teaspoon freshly ground pepper

Put the onion, carrots, potatoes, and celery in a large stockpot. Cover the vegetables with twice the amount of water. Add all the remaining ingredients. Bring to a boil, reduce heat to a low simmer, and cook, uncovered, for 1 hour, or until vegetables are soft and liquid is reduced by about one third. Strain through a colander into another pot. Store in the refrigerator for up to 3 days. To keep longer, bring to a boil every 3 days, or freeze for up to 3 months.

Makes about 8 cups

YIN-YANG POTATO SOUP

To create the yin-yang pattern, cut out a $1^1/_2$-inch strip of flexible cardboard about 6 to 8 inches long and cover it with aluminum foil (or use several thicknesses of aluminum foil to create a $1^1/_2$-inch strip). Hold the strip in the center of a soup bowl and bend to into an S shape. Enlist an extra set of hands to hold the strip in place, or tape it to the side of the bowl. Carefully ladle each soup into an opposite side of the divider, then lift the divider out.

2 tablespoons canola oil
1 small onion, finely chopped
2 or 3 white boiling potatoes, peeled and chopped
    (about 2 cups)
2 or 3 sweet potatoes, peeled and chopped (about 2
    cups)
$3^1/_2$ cups Vital Vegetable Stock (page 172)
1 teaspoon salt
$1/_8$ teaspoon freshly ground pepper
1 teaspoon packed brown sugar or a natural sweetener

$^1/_8$ teaspoon ground nutmeg

1 teaspoon minced fresh thyme, or $^1/_4$ teaspoon dried thyme

1 cup oat milk

Heat 1 tablespoon oil in each of 2 saucepans over medium heat. Add half the onion to each saucepan, cover, and cook for 5 minutes, or until softened. Add the white potatoes to one saucepan and the sweet potatoes to the other. Add half the stock to each saucepan, along with half the salt and pepper, stirring to combine. Add the brown sugar and nutmeg to the sweet potato mixture, and the thyme to the white potato mixture. Cover both saucepans, bring to a boil, then reduce heat to low. Cover and simmer until the potatoes are tender, about 30 minutes. Remove the saucepans from heat.

Put the white potato mixture in a blender or food processor and puree. Return the mixture to its saucepan. Repeat with the sweet potato mixture. Separately reheat both soups to a simmer over medium heat. Stir half of oat milk into each soup. Taste and adjust the seasoning. Heat again to serving temperature and carefully ladle each soup separately into bowls, using a piece of aluminum foil or cardboard as described above to replicate the yin-yang symbol. Garnish with a small dot of the alternate soup in the center of each kind of soup in each bowl.

Serves 4

Marvelous Matzo Soup

This new twist on a traditional favorite is a hearty broth chock-full of nutritious and colorful vegetables. Instead of the classic matzoh balls, this version floats quick-and-easy bite-sized matzoh crackers on the soup as a garnish.

My mama! . . . How wonderful the flavor, the aroma of her kitchen, her stories as she prepared the meal, her Christmas Rolls! I don't know why mine never turn out like hers, or why my tears flow so freely when I prepare them — perhaps I am as sensitive to onions as Tita, my great-aunt, who will go on living as long as there is someone who cooks her recipes.

— Laura Esquivel,
Like Water for Chocolate

1 tablespoon canola oil
1 large onion, chopped
2 carrots, chopped
1 celery stalk, chopped
2 cups shredded green cabbage
6 cups Vital Vegetable Stock (page 172)
1 teaspoon dried thyme
1 teaspoon dried basil
Salt and freshly ground pepper to taste
Bite-sized matzo crackers for garnish
1 tablespoon minced fresh parsley

Heat the oil in a large pot over medium heat and add the onion, carrots, celery, and cabbage. Stir the vegetables to coat with oil, cover, and cook until softened, about 10 minutes. Add the stock, thyme, basil, salt, and pepper. Bring to a boil, reduce heat to medium-low, and simmer for about 2 hours, stirring occasionally. Taste and adjust the seasoning. To serve, ladle the soup into bowls and float a few matzo crackers on top of each serving. Sprinkle with parsley. A basket of additional crackers may be served as an accompaniment.

Serves 6 to 8

FROM THE GARDEN GAZPACHO

Other than a salad, few dishes are as fresh tasting as a bowl of gazpacho made with fresh-picked vegetables. The vegetables should be chopped very finely, so it is best to begin this soup with a sharp knife and a meditative attitude. If you're pressed for time, however, the soup may also be prepared in a blender or food processor.

1 small onion, finely chopped
1 red or green bell pepper, seeded, deribbed, and

finely chopped
2 garlic cloves, minced
1 1/2 cups Vital Vegetable Stock (page 172)
1 1/2 cups V-8 juice
4 large ripe tomatoes, peeled, seeded, and chopped
1 small carrot, finely grated
2 cucumbers, peeled, seeded, and chopped
1 tablespoon olive oil
1 teaspoon salt
1/8 teaspoon cayenne pepper
1/4 cup finely chopped scallion
1/4 cup minced fresh parsley

In a large bowl, combine the onion, bell pepper, and garlic. Stir in the stock, V-8 juice, and tomatoes. Add the carrot and cucumber and stir in the olive oil. Season with the salt and cayenne. Cover and refrigerate for at least 1 hour to allow the flavors to blend. At serving time, taste and adjust the seasoning. Ladle into bowls and garnish with the scallion and parsley.

Serves 6

MELLOW WHITE MISO SOUP

The macrobiotic diet recommends having miso soup on a daily basis, as it is highly nutritious and is said to have properties that boost the immune system.

5 cups water
3 ounces mushrooms, sliced
1/4 cup chopped scallion
1/4 cup finely shredded carrot
1 tablespoon tamari sauce
1/4 cup white miso paste

Bring the water to a boil in a medium pot. Add the mushrooms, scallions, carrot, and tamari. Reduce heat to medium and simmer, uncovered, for 10 minutes, or until the vegetables soften. Reduce heat to low. Pour about $1/4$ cup of the hot soup mixture into a small bowl and add the miso paste, blending well. Stir the blended miso mixture back into the soup and simmer for 2 minutes, being careful not to boil. Taste and adjust the seasoning and serve.

Serves 4

> Dining is and always was a great artistic opportunity.
>
> — Frank Lloyd Wright

ENTRÉES

PENNE FOR YOUR THOUGHTS

Prepare this pasta dish mindfully. Think about each step of the process, including the ingredients and how they got to your kitchen. Visualize the pasta beginning as wheat growing in a field, and being harvested and milled and so on. Do the same as you chop the vegetables, visualizing each of them growing from seeds into plants, being harvested, and arriving at the present moment.

1 tablespoon olive oil
$1/2$ cup finely chopped onion
$1/2$ cup diced red bell pepper
3 ounces mushrooms, sliced
$1/4$ cup minced scallion
1 tablespoon minced garlic
2 tablespoons flour
2 $1/2$ cups soy milk, heated
1 tablespoon minced fresh basil, or $1/2$ teaspoon
    dried basil
1 teaspoon salt
$1/4$ teaspoon freshly ground pepper
1 cup diagonally cut asparagus pieces, steamed for 2
    minutes

1 cup sliced carrots, steamed for 2 minutes
1 pound penne pasta
2 tablespoons minced fresh parsley

Heat the oil in a large skillet over medium heat. Add the onion and sauté for 3 minutes. Add the bell pepper, mushrooms, scallion, and garlic and sauté 5 minutes. Stir in the flour and cook for 2 minutes. Reduce heat to low and gradually stir in the soy milk, basil, salt, and pepper. Cook, stirring, for 3 minutes. Add the asparagus and carrots and continue to cook for 3 minutes over low heat. Taste and adjust the seasoning.

Meanwhile, cook the pasta in a large pot of salted boiling water until al dente, about 12 minutes. Drain. Divide the pasta among the serving plates and top with the sauce. Sprinkle with the parsley.

Serves 4 to 6

SESAME BUCKWHEAT NOODLES AND MATCHSTICK VEGETABLES

Buckwheat soba noodles are available at natural foods stores and Asian markets. The tahini sauce is rich in calcium and protein. Matchstick vegetables are so-called because they are cut into fine julienne strips, about the size of a matchstick.

1 carrot, cut into matchsticks
12 green beans, trimmed and cut into matchsticks
1 turnip, cut into matchsticks
1 large garlic clove, chopped
$1/4$ cup fresh lemon juice
2 cups cooked chickpeas
$1/2$ cup tahini (sesame paste)
4 tablespoons tamari sauce
$1/8$ teaspoon cayenne pepper

2 tablespoons minced fresh parsley
1 pound buckwheat soba noodles

In a covered steamer over boiling water, lightly steam the carrot, green beans, and turnip until just tender, about 2 or 3 minutes. Set aside. In a blender or food processor, combine the garlic, lemon juice, chickpeas, tahini, tamari, cayenne, and 1 tablespoon of the parsley and process until smooth. Taste and adjust the seasoning. If a saltier flavor is desired, add more tamari and set aside.

Cook the noodles until tender according to the package directions. Meanwhile, with machine running, gradually add a small amount of warm water to the blender or food processor until the desired consistency of the sauce is reached. When the noodles are cooked, add the steamed vegetables to the pot and cook a minute or two to heat through. Drain. Toss the noodles and vegetables with the warm sauce. Garnish with the remaining parsley. Serve immediately.

Serves 4

GLOBAL PIZZA

Making global pizza can be enjoyed by the entire family. Use your toppings to make symbolic representations: the earth, with different vegetables representing the various land masses; the yin/yang symbol; or some other symbol that is important to you and your family.

1 cup unbleached all-purpose flour
$1/2$ cup whole wheat flour
$1/2$ teaspoon salt
1 teaspoon active dry yeast
$1/2$ cup warm (105° to 115°F water)
1 tablespoon olive oil
1 cup Fresh Tomato Sauce (page 93)

Every man should eat
and drink, and enjoy the
good of all his labor, it is
the gift of God.

— Ecclesiastes 3:13

1 cup shredded soy mozzarella cheese
Sautéed mushrooms, sliced olives, roasted red pepper strips, artichoke hearts, etc., for topping

In a food processor, combine the flours and salt using several on/off pulses. In a small bowl, dissolve the yeast in the water and let sit for 5 minutes. Add the olive oil. With machine running, pour the yeast mixture through the feed tube and process to form a dough ball, about 1 minute. Turn out onto a lightly floured surface and knead until smooth, about 1 minute. Transfer the dough to a large oiled bowl, coating the top of the dough with oil as well. Cover with plastic wrap and a dry cloth and let rise in warm area until doubled, about $1\,^1/_2$ hours.

Preheat the oven to 425°F. Punch the dough down. On a floured surface, roll the dough out to a 12-inch circle. Place on a lightly floured pizza pan or baking sheet. Spread tomato sauce on the dough, leaving a $^1/_2$-inch border around the edge. Sprinkle the soy mozzarella over the sauce. Add your toppings of choice. Bake for 20 minutes, or until the crust is golden brown.

Makes one 12-inch pizza; serves 2 to 4

NORIMAKI SUSHI

Sushi means "rice sandwich" in Japanese. The filling doesn't need to include raw fish. Roasted, sushi seaweed, or nori, is available in Asian markets and many supermarkets, as are sticky rice, wasabi paste, and pickled ginger.

2 cups sticky (glutinous) rice
$^3/_4$ teaspoon sea salt
6 roasted nori sheets
2 tablespoons wasabi paste (hot Japanese horseradish)
12 carrot strips, $^1/_4$-inch thick by 4-inches long, blanched

6 cucumber strips, $^1/_4$-inch thick by 4 inches long
6 avocado strips, $^1/_4$-inch thick by 4 inches long
Pickled ginger for garnish
Tamari sauce for dipping

Combine the rice with $2^1/_2$ cups of water and salt in a saucepan. Cover and bring to a boil, then reduce heat to low and cook for 20 minutes. Remove from heat and allow to stand, covered, for 10 minutes. Spread the rice in a wide, shallow bowl and allow to cool.

Place 1 sheet of nori on a bamboo sushi mat or a cloth napkin. Spread $^3/_4$ cup rice evenly on the nori, all the way to the edge on the sides, and leaving a $^1/_2$-inch border at the top and bottom. Spread $^1/_2$ teaspoon wasabi paste along the length of rice nearest you. Line 2 strips of carrot end to end on top of the wasabi and place 2 cucumber strips parallel to the carrot strips.

Beginning at the end nearest you, start rolling up the mat or napkin, pressing firmly against the nori to enclose the filling, all the while keeping the end of the mat or napkin from rolling into the sushi. Continue rolling up to the top. Wet the end of the exposed nori with a little water to seal the roll. Gently squeeze the mat or napkin around the sushi roll and remove. Using a sharp knife, cut across the center of the sushi roll, then cut each half into thirds to create 6 slices. Arrange on a platter, one cut-side down.

Repeat with remaining nori, rice, carrots, and cucumber to make 2 more rolls, using carrots and avocado for remaining 3 rolls. Garnish the platter with pickled ginger, a small mound of wasabi, and a small dipping bowl of tamari. Serve with chopsticks.

Makes 36 pieces

BAKED WINTER SQUASH WITH POMEGRANATE-WALNUT SAUCE

If kabocha squash is unavailable, substitute any sweet winter squash, such as butternut or acorn. This attractive dish makes a great main course for Thanksgiving dinner.

> Eating in a hurried or unconscious way, as so many of us have learned to do, is like receiving a love letter from the Earth but never taking the time to carefully read it.
>
> — John Robbins, *May All be Fed*

2 small kabocha squash
1 tablespoon canola oil
1 onion, chopped
1 garlic clove, minced
6 ounces mushrooms, sliced
$^1/_2$ cup raisins
2 teaspoons minced fresh ginger
$^1/_4$ teaspoon ground cardamom
$^1/_4$ teaspoon ground cinnamon
$^1/_2$ teaspoon salt
$^1/_4$ teaspoon freshly ground pepper
3 cups Brown Rice with Love (page 21)
$^1/_4$ cup chopped walnuts
$^1/_2$ cup Vital Vegetable Stock (page 172)
Pomegranate-Walnut Sauce (page 194)

Preheat the oven to 375°F. Halve the kabocha squash and scoop out the seeds. Place the squash halves cut-side down in a shallow baking dish, add $^1/_2$ inch water, cover tightly with a lid or aluminum foil, and bake for 30 minutes, or until tender. Remove from the oven and carefully turn the squash over. Let cool slightly.

While the squash is baking, heat the oil in a large skillet over medium heat. Add the onion and garlic, cover, and cook, stirring occasionally, until the onion is translucent, about 10 minutes. Add the mushrooms, raisins, ginger, cardamom, cinnamon, salt, and pepper. Sauté, uncovered, until the mushrooms are soft, about 5 minutes. Remove from heat. Stir in the rice, walnuts, and stock. Let cool briefly.

Divide the stuffing equally among squash halves. Return the baking dish to the oven and bake, uncovered, for 20 minutes. Serve topped with Pomegranate-Walnut Sauce.

Serves 4

I feel a recipe is only a theme, which an intelligent cook can play each time with a variation.

— Madame Benoit

DHARMA BURGERS

From the cooking of the lentils and brown rice to the grinding of almonds and grating of carrots and onions, the resulting burgers are true labors of love. Serve with Magic Mushroom Sauce (page 194), or on a toasted whole-grain roll with all the trimmings.

$1/2$ cup dried lentils
1 cup Brown Rice with Love (page 21)
$1/2$ cup ground almonds
$1/4$ cup grated carrot, steamed for 2 minutes
$1/4$ cup grated onion
$1/2$ teaspoon salt
$1/2$ teaspoon chili powder
$1/8$ teaspoon cayenne pepper
$3/4$ cup dried bread crumbs
2 tablespoons canola oil, plus more as needed

Place the lentils in a saucepan with 3 cups of cold water, cover, and bring to a boil. Reduce heat to low and simmer for 25 to 30 minutes or until tender.

In a large bowl, combine the lentils and all the remaining ingredients, except the bread crumbs and oil, until well mixed. Shape the mixture into 6 patties. Coat with the bread crumbs. Heat the oil in a large skillet over medium-high heat. Cook the patties for about 4 minutes on each side, or until golden brown. Add more oil to the skillet as needed.

Serves 6

AUTUMN HARVEST VEGETABLE PUDDING

Comfort food at its best: the homey goodness of savory bread pudding filled with the delicious taste of autumn vegetables. This one-dish meal can be prepared in advance. Simply heat and eat when ready.

2 tablespoons canola oil
1 $1/2$ cups finely chopped onions
1 teaspoon minced garlic
1 pound soft tofu, drained and crumbled
2 cups soy milk
$1/2$ cup shredded soy mozzarella
1 tablespoon Dijon mustard
1 teaspoon ground sage
$3/4$ teaspoon salt
$1/8$ teaspoon freshly ground pepper
6 cups whole-grain bread cubes
1 cup winter squash, diced
1 cup carrots, diced
1 cup sliced mushrooms

Preheat oven to 350°F. Heat the oil in a large skillet over low heat. Add the onions, cover, and cook for 5 minutes. Add the garlic and sauté 2 minutes. In a bowl, combine the tofu, 1 cup of the soy milk, the soy mozzarella, mustard, sage, salt, and pepper and mix well. Blend in the onion mixture. Stir in the remaining 1 cup soy milk. Lightly oil a large shallow baking dish and put the bread in it. Pour the tofu mixture over the bread, using a fork to distribute the ingredients evenly. Let soak until the liquid is absorbed, about 30 minutes.

Meanwhile, steam the squash for 6 to 8 minutes or until soft and reserve. Steam the carrots for 3 to 5 minutes or until soft and add to the squash. Then lightly steam the mushrooms for 1 minute and add to reserved squash and carrots. Stir the reserved mushrooms, carrots, and squash into the bread mixture. Bake the pudding for 30 minutes. Increase the oven temperature to 375°F . Continue baking until puffy and lightly browned, about 10 minutes. Let stand a few minutes before serving.

Serves 8

FIVE-FLAVOR TOFU WITH SAKE-ORANGE SAUCE

A symphony of flavors infuse the basic goodness of tofu, rich in calcium and protein.

1 tablespoon five-spice powder
$1/8$ teaspoon cayenne pepper
1 pound firm tofu, drained and cut into 1-inch slices
1 tablespoon canola oil
2 cups Vital Vegetable Stock (page 172)
2 tablespoons grated orange zest
2 tablespoons sake or dry white wine
Salt and freshly ground pepper to taste
Brown Rice with Love (page 21)
1 tablespoon chopped fresh cilantro

In a shallow bowl, combine the five-spice powder and cayenne. Sprinkle the spice mixture evenly on the tofu pieces. Heat the oil in a large skillet over medium heat. Add the tofu and cook until browned on each side, about 6 minutes total. Remove from the skillet and keep warm. Add the stock to the skillet and cook over medium-high heat until reduced to 1 cup. Add the orange zest and sake or wine and bring to a simmer. Return the tofu to the pan to heat briefly. Add the salt and pepper. Serve over rice, sprinkled with cilantro.

Serves 4 to 6

The secret of good cooking is, first, having a love of it . . . If you're convinced cooking is drudgery, you're never going to be good at it, and you might as well warm up something frozen.

— James Beard

GAIA VEGETABLE POT PIE

The comfort of Mother Nature's finest: a flaky crust topping a bounty of vegetables swimming in a creamy sauce.

FOR THE FILLING:
1 cup diced carrots
1 cup finely chopped onions
2 cups cooked chickpeas
1 cup frozen peas, thawed
1 tablespoon minced fresh parsley
2 tablespoons canola oil
3 tablespoons unbleached all-purpose flour
1 cup Vital Vegetable Stock (page 172)
1 cup soy milk
$1/2$ teaspoon salt
$1/8$ teaspoon finely ground pepper

FOR THE CRUST:
1 cup unbleached all-purpose flour
$1/2$ cup whole wheat flour
$1/8$ teaspoon salt
4 tablespoons soy margarine
2 tablespoons ice water

To make the filling: Put the carrots, onions, chickpeas, peas, and parsley in a lightly oiled casserole dish. Heat the oil in a medium saucepan over low heat. Stir in the flour and cook, stirring constantly, for 3 minutes. Gradually add the stock and soy milk, stirring until smooth. Bring to a boil, stirring. Remove from heat. Add the salt and pepper. Pour the sauce over the vegetables in the casserole dish.

To make the crust: Preheat the oven to 350°F. Combine the flour and salt in a food processor, using the steel blade. Add the soy margarine and process until the mixture resembles coarse crumbs. With the machine running, gradually add the water, processing to blend. Roll the dough out on a lightly floured surface to a $1/4$-inch thickness, shaped to the size of the casserole dish. Carefully place the crust over the filled casserole, crimping the edges to seal. Bake for 40 minutes, or until lightly browned.

Serves 6

THE WHOLE ENCHILADA

Try this make-ahead version of the classic Mexican favorite for a quick weeknight supper.

1 tablespoon canola oil
$1/2$ cup finely chopped onion
$1/4$ cup finely chopped red or green bell pepper
1 teaspoon minced garlic
$1 1/2$ teaspoons chili powder
$1/2$ cup water
$1 1/2$ cups tomato salsa
1 cup tofu sour cream
2 cups cooked pinto beans, chopped
Eight 8-inch flour tortillas

Preheat oven to 350°F. Lightly oil a 9 -by-13-inch baking dish.

Heat the oil in a large saucepan over medium heat. Add the onion, bell pepper, and garlic. Cover and cook for 5 minutes, or until softened. Stir in the chili powder, water, and salsa and cook, stirring, until slightly thickened. Remove from heat and add the tofu sour cream. Combine 2 cups of the sauce with the beans. Spoon about $1/3$ cup of the bean mixture onto each tortilla and roll up. Arrange the filled tortillas in the prepared baking dish. Top with the remaining sauce, cover, and bake for 25 minutes. Uncover and bake 5 minutes longer.

Serves 6 to 8

In the childhood memories of every good cook, there's a large kitchen, a warm stove, a simmering pot and a mom.

— Barbara Costikkyan

THANKFUL HOLIDAY ROAST

This recipe calls for a large piece of raw seitan (wheat meat), which is best when made with Seitan Quick Mix by Arrowhead Mills. It makes short work of the lengthy seitan-making process. If the "quick-mix" is unavailable, omit the seitan, and bake the stuffing in a loaf pan or casserole or use it to stuff a winter squash.

1 pound uncooked seitan
$1/2$ cup tamari sauce
2 tablespoons canola oil
1 small onion, finely chopped
8 ounces vegetarian sausage, cooked and crumbled
5 mushrooms, chopped
$1/4$ teaspoon dried thyme
Salt and freshly ground pepper to taste
4 cups fresh bread crumbs
Water as needed
$1 1/2$ cups Magic Mushroom Sauce (page 194)

Prepare raw seitan according to package directions. Marinate the raw seitan in the tamari sauce for at least 1 hour or overnight. To bake, preheat oven to 375°F. Oil a shallow baking pan.

Heat the oil in a large skillet over medium heat. Add the onion, cover, and cook for 5 minutes, or until softened. Stir in the sausage, mushrooms, thyme, salt, and pepper and cook for 5 minutes, stirring frequently. Transfer the mixture to a large bowl. Add the bread crumbs and blend well, adding a small amount of water if the mixture is too dry. Set aside.

Drain the seitan and reserve the marinade. Roll out seitan with a rolling pin to a $1/4$-inch thickness. Spread the surface with the stuffing. Roll up jelly roll fashion. Place seam-side down in prepared pan. Pierce with a fork in several places. Pour the reserved marinade over the roast. Bake, uncovered, for 30 to 40 minutes, basting every 10 minutes. The roast is done when the surface is firm, browned, and glossy. Remove from oven, and cut into $^1/_2$ inch-slices with a serrated knife. Serve with the mushroom sauce.

Serves 8

OH, YOU BEAUTIFUL DAL

This classic Indian dish can be a meal in itself or a companion to a curried dish. Dals can be made with a variety of different legumes, such as lentils or peas, depending on preference. Garam masala is an Indian spice mixture used to make curries. If unavailable, use regular curry powder or paste.

1 $^1/_4$ cups dried lentils
1 tablespoon canola oil
1 teaspoon or more garam masala
1 onion, finely chopped
1 garlic clove, finely minced
1 tablespoon minced fresh ginger
1 cup chopped tomatoes
Salt to taste
$^1/_4$ teaspoon cayenne pepper
$^1/_4$ teaspoon ground coriander
$^1/_8$ teaspoon ground turmeric
1 tablespoon chopped fresh cilantro

Put the lentils in a saucepan with 4 cups of water and bring to a boil. Reduce heat to medium-low and simmer, covered for 30 minutes, or until soft. Drain and set aside.

Heat the oil in a skillet over medium heat. Add the garam masala and onion and sauté until the onion begins to soften, about 5 minutes. Stir in the garlic, ginger, tomatoes, salt, cayenne, coriander, and turmeric and cook until the vegetables have softened, about 10 minutes. Combine the onion mixture with the cooked lentils, transfer to a serving dish, and sprinkle with chopped cilantro.

Serves 4

SIDE DISHES

PEAS IN THE POD

Called *edamame* in Japan, this dish of soybeans served in their bright green pods is simplicity itself. Soybeans in the pod are often found fresh or frozen in Asian markets. The frozen variety is usually preboiled and simply needs defrosting at room temperature or under hot running water before serving. Served as an appetizer, this "pick-up food" is eaten by placing the cut-end of the pod between the teeth, and pushing the beans out with your thumb and forefinger from the opposite end, allowing the luscious beans to fall into your mouth. Be sure to have an empty bowl placed on the table to discard the empty pods.

1 pound fresh or frozen soybeans in the pod
Coarse salt for sprinkling

If using fresh soybeans cook them in a pot of salted boiling water until tender, about 15 minutes. Drain and let cool to room temperature. If using frozen, preboiled soy beans, defrost. With a sharp knife cut the stem off each pod. Put in a serving bowl and garnish with a sprinkling of coarse salt.

Serves 8

HEAVEN AND EARTH BEETS

The vibrant colors of tender young beets with their iron-rich greens are a dazzling addition to any table. By using both parts of the beets, that which is grown both above and below the ground, you are getting all the vital nutrients they have to offer.

8 small beets with greens attached
Tamari sauce for sprinkling
Mirin for sprinkling (optional)

Trim off the beet roots and discard. Cut off the beet greens, leaving about $1/2$ inch of stems on each beet; reserve the greens. Scrub the beets to remove any dirt. Cook the beets in a pot of boiling water for about 15 minutes, or until just tender. Drain to cool under running water. With your hands, slip off the beet skin. Set the beets aside.

Wash the reserved greens well. Cook in a pot of salted boiling water for 4 to 5 minutes, or until tender. Drain and cool under running water. Cut each beet into $1/4$-inch dice and put in a shallow bowl. Chop the leaves and arrange them in a ring around the mound of beets. Sprinkle with tamari and the optional mirin. Serve at room temperature.

Serves 4

> Those who are one in food are one in life.
>
> — Malagasy saying

STEAMED VEGETABLE BUNDLES

These lovely bundles of colorful vegetables tied with ribbons of scallions make a beautiful adornment for the Thankful Holiday Roast platter, or a garnish for any other special-occasion dinner.

2 carrots
2 parsnips

12 green beans, trimmed
4 scallion greens or chives
Chopped fresh herbs (optional)
Salt and freshly ground pepper to taste

Cut the carrots and parsnips into strips the same size as the green beans. Steam the vegetables separately over boiling water in a covered pot until just tender, about 2 to 3 minutes. Gather the vegetables into 4 bundles consisting of 3 or 4 of pieces each vegetable per bundle. Steam the scallion greens or chives for 1 minute. Tie each bundle with a steamed scallion or chive.

Just before serving, reheat in a covered skillet with a small amount of water. Add some chopped fresh herbs, if desired, and salt and pepper.

Serves 4

Sauces and Dressings

Pickled-Ginger Dressing

This palate-pleasing dressing can be used on a salad of mixed greens or as a dipping sauce for norimakis (page 180), crudités, or spring rolls (page 18).

1 large scallion, minced
1 garlic clove, minced
2 tablespoons toasted sesame oil
2 tablespoons tamari sauce
$1/4$ cup rice vinegar
$1/2$ cup pickled ginger, drained
1 tablespoon sesame seeds

Combine all the ingredients in a blender or food processor

and mix until thoroughly blended. Cover and refrigerate for at least 2 hours or up to 1 week.

Makes about 1 cup

TAMARIND-PLUM DIPPING SAUCE

This transcendent sauce is especially good with samosas, pakoras, egg rolls, or steamed dumplings, but it can add an exotic nuance to many other dishes as well. Use your imagination and pair it with something unexpected, like steamed vegetables or stir-fried tofu. Tamarind paste is available in Indian markets or specialty food shops.

$1/4$ cup apple juice
1 cup canned plums, drained and pitted
1 tablespoon fresh lemon juice
2 tablespoons tamarind paste
$1/8$ teaspoon cayenne pepper
$1/8$ teaspoon ground coriander
$1/8$ teaspoon ground cinnamon

In a blender or food processor, combine all the ingredients and until smooth. Transfer to a small bowl, cover, and refrigerate for at least 2 hours or up to 1 week.

Makes about 1 cup; serves 4 to 6

MAGIC MUSHROOM SAUCE

Mushrooms puréed in vegetable stock produce a rich velvety sauce that belies its ease of preparation. Serve over pasta, grains, mashed potatoes, or serve with the Thankful Holiday Roast (page 188).

2 1/2 cups Vital Vegetable Stock (page 172)
8 ounces fresh white mushrooms, halved
1 tablespoon tamari sauce
1 tablespoon minced fresh parsley
1/8 teaspoon dried thyme
Salt and freshly ground pepper to taste
1 tablespoon arrowroot mixed with 1 tablespoon water

Combine the stock and mushrooms in a medium saucepan and bring to a boil. Reduce heat to medium and simmer until the mushrooms soften, about 5 minutes. Transfer the mushroom mixture to a blender and puree with the tamari, parsley, thyme, salt, and pepper. Return to the saucepan and heat almost to boiling. Whisk in the arrowroot mixture and stir until thickened. Taste and adjust the seasoning. If not using sauce immediately, it may be cooled, covered, and stored in the refrigerator for 3 to 4 days.

Makes about 3 1/2 cups

POMEGRANATE-WALNUT SAUCE

Pomegranate juice is available in natural foods stores, or you can make your own by rolling the fruit on a hard surface to break up the membranes to yield more juice. Then, poke a hole in one end of the fruit and squeeze the juice into a container. In addition to enhancing stuffed squash, this sauce is a great way to liven up sautéed tofu cutlets, baked eggplant, or grilled mushrooms.

1 tablespoon canola oil
1 large onion, chopped
1/4 teaspoon ground turmeric
1 cup ground walnuts

2 cups Vital Vegetable Stock (page 172)
$^1/_2$ teaspoon salt
$^1/_8$ teaspoon freshly ground pepper
$^1/_2$ cup pomegranate juice
$^1/_4$ cup fresh lemon juice
2 tablespoons tomato paste
$^1/_4$ cup sugar or a natural sweetener

Heat the oil in a large skillet or saucepan over medium heat. Add the onion and turmeric and cook, covered, for 5 minutes. Add the walnuts, stock, salt, and pepper and bring to a boil. Reduce heat and simmer, covered, for 15 minutes. In a bowl, combine the pomegranate juice with the lemon juice, tomato paste, and sugar or sweetener. Add the mixture to the saucepan, stirring gently to mix. Simmer, uncovered for 15 minutes longer, or until desired consistency is reached. If not using immediately, sauce can be cooled and stored in the refrigerator in a covered container for 3 to 5 days.

Makes about 3 cups; serves 6 to 8

DESSERTS

CHOCOLATE MOUSSE-COUS CAKE

It looks like cheesecake, has a texture somewhere between rice pudding and bread pudding, and tastes like chocolate. What could be better? It's even good for you.

1 cup soft silken tofu
4 ounces semi-sweet chocolate, melted
1 teaspoon vanilla extract
2 tablespoons sugar or a natural sweetener
1 $^1/_2$ cups apple juice
1 tablespoon unsweetened cocoa powder

Pinch of salt

1 cup couscous

$1/_2$ cup white or dark chocolate shavings or curls for garnish

In a blender or food processor, combine the tofu, melted chocolate, vanilla, and 1 tablespoon of the sugar or sweetener. Blend thoroughly until well combined. Cover and refrigerate. In a small saucepan, combine the apple juice, cocoa, remaining 1 tablespoon sugar, and salt. Bring to a boil, reduce heat to low, and add the couscous. Cover and simmer for 2 minutes, then turn off the heat and let sit, covered, for 5 minutes. Spread the couscous mixture in a lightly oiled 8-inch round springform pan, pressing the couscous firmly and evenly over the bottom and up the sides of the pan. Spread the tofu mixture evenly over the couscous. Sprinkle with chocolate shavings or curls. Refrigerate for at least 2 hours or overnight before slicing.

Serves 8

APPLE-WALNUT STIR-FRY PIE

All the flavor of apple pie in a fraction of the time. For an even faster dessert, try this warm spicy apple mixture over vanilla ice cream, and garnish with a cookie.

One 12-ounce package fat-free fruit-sweetened oatmeal cookies

1 tablespoon water

$1/_2$ teaspoon fresh lemon juice

3 Granny Smith apples, peeled, cored, and thinly sliced

$1/_4$ cup walnut pieces, lightly toasted

3 tablespoons brown rice syrup or barley malt

$1/_4$ teaspoon ground cinnamon

Break the cookies into a blender or food processor and process into crumbs. Press the crumbs into a lightly oiled 8-inch pie plate. Refrigerate.

Combine the water and lemon juice in a large skillet over medium heat. Add the apple slices, cover, and cook for 2 minutes, or until slightly softened. Add the walnuts, brown rice syrup or barley malt, and cinnamon. Increase heat to medium-high and stir-fry until the apples are slightly glazed, about 2 minutes.

Remove the crust from the refrigerator and spoon the apple mixture into it. Let cool slightly, then cut into wedges and serve with vanilla ice cream, frozen yogurt, or nondairy frozen dessert.

Serves 6

The most indispensable ingredient of all good home cooking: love for those you are cooking for.

— Sophia Loren

EID PUDDING

Eid al-Fitr is the meal served after Ramadan, a time of fasting. Many traditional foods are served at this feast, one of which is this sweet vermicelli pudding. Try it next time you want a interesting change from rice pudding.

2 cups broken vermicelli noodles
2 cups water
$1/2$ cup soy milk
$1/4$ cup sugar or a natural sweetener
$1/4$ cup sliced almonds
$1/4$ cup golden raisins
1 teaspoon vanilla extract
Sliced dried apricots and ground cinnamon for garnish

Put the vermicelli in a saucepan with the water and bring to a boil. Reduce heat, stirring occasionally to keep the vermicelli from sticking. Cook over low heat for about 8 minutes, or until the water evaporates. Remove from heat. Add the soy milk, sugar or sweetener, almonds, raisins, and vanilla. Stir until the ingredients are well combined. Transfer to a serving dish and smooth the top. Garnish with apricots and sprinkle with cinnamon.

Serves 4 to 6

CHOCOLATE SILK ROAD PIE

This variation of chocolate silk pie is made with silken tofu. It has all the flavor of the original, with no cholesterol, plus the nutritional benefits of soy protein.

FOR THE CRUST:
1 1/2 cups fruit-sweetened chocolate cookie crumbs
     (about 6 to 8 cookies)
3 tablespoons soy margarine, melted

FOR THE FILLING:
2 cups soft silken tofu
3/4 cup sugar or a natural sweetener
1/2 cup unsweetened cocoa powder
1 teaspoon vanilla extract

To make the crust: Put the cookie crumbs in the bottom of a lightly oiled 9-inch pie plate. Add the melted soy margarine, and toss with a fork to blend. Press the crumb mixture into the bottom and up the sides of the pie plate and bake for 5 minutes to set. Remove from oven and let cool.

In a blender or food processor, combine the tofu, sweetener, cocoa powder, and vanilla and process until smooth. Pour the filling mixture into the crust. Refrigerate for at least 2 hours, or until set, before serving.

Serves 8

BEVERAGES

RUBY SIPPER COOLER

Click your heels three times before drinking this luscious fruity drink. You'll know you're not in Kansas anymore. It's a delightful way to enjoy fresh berries.

$1/2$ cup fresh raspberries
$1/2$ cup fresh strawberries
$1/2$ cup cranberry juice
1 cup frozen strawberries
1 frozen banana, cut into chunks

Combine the raspberries and the fresh strawberries in a blender with the cranberry juice. Blend to a purée, about 1 minute. Add the frozen strawberries and banana chunks. Blend until smooth, about 1 minute longer.

Serves 2

OPEN SESAME SMOOTHIE

This rich and creamy concoction is loaded with vitamins and minerals — and it tastes great. Try it for a quick and easy breakfast or a between-meal pick-me-up.

1 tablespoon tahini (sesame paste)
1 tablespoon barley malt or brown rice syrup
1 cup orange juice
1 frozen banana, cut into chunks
Ground cinnamon for sprinkling

Combine the tahini, barley malt or rice syrup, and orange juice in a blender and blend until well combined, about 1 minute. Add the banana and blend until smooth, about 1 minute longer. Pour into a tall glass and sprinkle with cinnamon.

A smiling face is half the meal.

— Latvian proverb

Serves 1

LASSI COME HOME

Mango lassi gets a makeover with tofu and soy milk. Yogurt may be substituted for a more classic version.

    1 cup diced mango
    $1/2$ cup soft tofu, drained
    $1/4$ cup soy milk
    1 cup mango juice, frozen into cubes
    Ground cardamom for sprinkling

In a blender, combine the diced mango, tofu, soy milk, and frozen mango juice cubes. Blend until smooth, about 1 minute. Pour into 2 glasses and sprinkle with cardamom.

Serves 2

SAMPLE MENUS

The following menu suggestions can be used to create meals that can serve a variety of functions, ranging from everyday meals to meals for celebrations. The menus from the first six chapters are listed first, followed by menus based on the recipes in chapter 7.

Use the menus for special holiday dining. For example, the Thanksgiving Dinner for Anytime is a great year-round menu. The

Asian Influence, Winter Wonderland, and New Tradition dinners, are ideal for day-to-day meals but are perfect for intimate entertaining as well. The Let's Party menu is a fun food buffet that is great for parties and other casual gatherings. You can of course, mix and match these and other recipes to create your own centered Cuisine menus.

MENUS FROM THE CHAPTERS

A Meal to Feel the Life Force
First-Sign-of-Spring Rolls
Peanut Sauce
Favoring Curry
Brown Rice with Love
Grilled Pineapple with Mango Coulis

Dinner for Balance in the Senses
Ecstasy Jade Soup
Golden Sun Sauté
Samhadi-Loves-You Banana-Berry Pudding

Menu from a Tiny Herb Garden
Pesto de Resistance (or Pesto, Two)
Summer Solstice Salad
Goddess Green Herb Dressing

A Meal for Change
Field Greens with Lemon-Mint Vinaigrette
Everyone's Favorite Lasagna
"Say Cheese" Cake

A Dinner of New Traditions
Harira (Ramadan Soup)
Hoppin' John
Haroset
Sticky Rice Balls (Tang Yuan)

In every heart Thou art
hidden; In every heart
burns Thy light.

— the *Adi Granth,* sacred
scripture of Sikhism

A Celebration Dinner

Potage du Soleil

Celebration Salmagundi

Eight-Treasure Rice

Create-Your-Own-Reality Sundaes

ADDITIONAL MENUS USING THE REMAINING RECIPES

A Thanksgiving Dinner for Anytime

Yin-Yang Potato Soup

Thankful Holiday Roast

Magic Mushroom Sauce

Steamed Vegetable Bundles

Apple-Walnut Stir-Fry Pie

Asian Influence

Mellow White Miso Soup

Norimaki Sushi

Salad with Pickled-Ginger Dressing

Sesame Buckwheat Noodles and Matchstick Vegetables

A Winter Wonderland

Baked Winter Squash with Pomegranate-Walnut Sauce

Autumn Harvest Vegetable Pudding

Chocolate Mousse-Cous Cake

International Savors

Marvelous Matzo Soup

Gaia Vegetable Pot Pie

Heaven-and-Earth Beets

Eid Pudding

Let's Party

From-the-Garden Gazpacho

Global Pizza

Norimaki Sushi

Peas in the Pod
Chocolate Silk Road Pie
Ruby Sipper Coolers

*The active awareness that what one eats comes from Nature's
bountiful earth rather than from a grocery shelf or
fast-food bag honors Mother Nature. The Ten Commandments
say to honor our mother and father. To me,
this includes Mother Nature, whom I refer to as the Earthly
Mother, and God, the Heavenly Father.*

— Gabriel Cousens, M.D., *Conscious Eating*

APPENDIX I: Pantry List for a Centered Cuisine

Below is a sample grocery list that can serve as a guide to stocking a basic vegetarian pantry. You may wish to refer to it when compiling your weekly shopping list. When you plan your menus, you can do a check list of the ingredients in each recipe you are using to see what you have on hand and what you need to buy. Do this each week, adding a few new ingredients each time. Before long, you will have a well-stocked "centered" pantry. Buy grains and beans in bulk if possible, as it is more economical and environmentally sound. Buy as much as you can store in large, decorative glass jars.

Produce
Seasonal vegetables
Seasonal fruit
Salad greens
Onions
Garlic
Carrots
Celery
Lemons/limes
Fresh herbs
Dried fruits: raisins, dates, prunes, apples

Grain Products
Brown rice
Millet
Couscous
Pastas
Popcorn
Oatmeal
Breakfast cereals
Whole-grain breads
Whole-grain crackers
Tortillas
Pita bread
Flours
Seitan Quick Mix

Dried Beans
Adzuki beans
Lentils
Split peas
Black beans
Pinto beans

Soy Foods
Tofu, regular
Tofu, silken
Tempeh
Soy milk
Miso paste
Vegetarian "cold cuts"
TVP (textured vegetable protein)

Condiments
Tamari sauce
Salsa
Chutney
Vinegars
Tahini
Teriyaki sauce
Mustard
Tomato paste
Curry pastes
Chili sauce
Nutritional yeast
Sea vegetables (kombu, nori, kelp, etc.)
Vegetable broth cubes
Vegan mayonnaise
Olives, capers, pickles

Oils
Olive oil
Toasted sesame oil
Canola oil

Convenience Foods
Frozen
Veggie burgers
Tofu hot dogs
Ground beef alternatives
Seitan
Frozen non-dairy desserts
Vegetables: artichoke hearts, peas
Canned
Chickpeas and other beans
Tomato products

Artichoke hearts

Nuts and Seeds
Almonds
Sesame seeds
Sunflower seeds
Pecans
Peanuts
Walnuts
Nut butters

Beverages
Organic coffee
Herbal teas
Fruit juice
Vegetable juice
Grain beverage
Spring water
Rice milk
Oat milk

Spices
Dry mustard
Thyme
Cayenne
Black peppercorns
Sea salt
Chili powder
Basil
Oregano
Cinnamon
Allspice
Nutmeg

Sweeteners
Maple syrup
Brown rice syrup
Barley malt
Sucanat

APPENDIX II: Resources Directory

Dietary Organizations

AYURVEDA

CHOPRA CENTER FOR WELL-BEING
7630 Fay Avenue
La Jolla, CA 92037
(800) 424-6772
website: www.chopra.com

HEALING TAO CENTER
P.O. Box 1194
Huntington, NY 11743
Phone: (800) 497-1017
Fax: (516) 368-7413
website: www.healing-tao.com

MACROBIOTIC

THE KUSHI FOUNDATION
17 Station Street
Brookline Village, MA 02147
(800) 975-8744

GEORGE OHSAWA
MACROBIOTIC FOUNDATION
1999 Myers Street
Oroville, CA 95966
(530) 533-7702

EAST WEST CENTER
INSTITUTE FOR MACROBIOTIC STUDIES
11215 Hannum Avenue
Culver City, CA 90230
(310) 398-2228

VEGETARIAN

AMERICAN VEGAN SOCIETY
501 Old Harding Highway
Malaga, NJ 08328
(609) 694-2887

NORTH AMERICAN VEGETARIAN
SOCIETY
P.O. Box 72
Dolgeville, NY 13329
(518) 568-7970
e-mail: NAVS@telenet.net

VEGETARIAN RESOURCE GROUP
P.O. Box 1463
Baltimore, MD 21203
(410) 366-8343

Environmental Organizations

BUDDHIST PEACE FELLOWSHIP
P.O. Box 4650
Berkeley, CA 94704
(510) 655-6169

THE COALITION ON THE
ENVIRONMENT AND JEWISH LIFE
443 Park Avenue South,
Eleventh Floor
New York, NY 10016-7322
(212) 684-6950, ext. 210
e-mail: coejl@aol.com
website: www.jtsa.edu/org/coejl

EARTHSAVE
600 Distillery Commons,
Suite 200
Louisville, KY 40206
(502) 589-7676
e-mail: EarthSave@aol.com
website: www.earthsave.org

FARM SANCTUARY
P.O. Box 150
Watkins Glen, NY 148891
(607) 583-2225

FRIENDS OF THE EARTH
1025 Vermont Avenue, Suite 300
Washington, DC 20005
(202) 783-7400

THE FUND FOR ANIMALS
200 West 57th Street
New York, NY 10023
(212) 246-2096

GREENPEACE USA
1436 U Street, NW
Washington, DC 20009
(202) 462-8817
website: www.greenpeaceusa.org

INTERFAITH COUNCIL FOR THE
Protection of Animals and Nature
3691 Tuxedo Road
Atlanta, GA 30305
(404) 814-1371

THE ORION SOCIETY
195 Main Street
Great Barrington, MA 01230
(413) 528-4422
e-mail: orion@orionsociety.org
website: www.orionsociety.org

PETA (PEOPLE FOR THE ETHICAL
TREATMENT OF ANIMALS)
501 Front Street
Norfolk, VA 23510
(757) 622-7382

RAINFOREST ACTION NETWORK
221 Pine Street, Suite 500
San Francisco, CA 94104
(415) 398-4404

UNITED STATES CATHOLIC
CONFERENCE
ENVIRONMENTAL JUSTICE PROGRAM
3711 4th Street, NE
Washington, DC 20017
(202) 541-3182
e-mail: spak@ncbusc.org

Health Organizations

AMERICAN DIETETIC ASSOCIATION
216 West Jackson Boulevard,
Suite 800
Chicago, IL 60606
(312) 899-0040

AMERICAN HOLISTIC MEDICAL
ASSOCIATION
4101 Lake Boone Trail, No. 201
Raleigh, NC 27607
(919) 787-5146

CARE
151 Ellis Street. NE
Atlanta, GA 30303
(800) 422-7385

CATHOLIC RELIEF SERVICES
P.O. Box 17090
Baltimore, MD 21203-7090
(410) 625-2220

CENTER FOR SCIENCE IN THE PUBLIC
INTEREST
1875 Connecticut Avenue, NW,
Suite 300
Washington, DC 20009
(202) 332-9110

CHURCH WORLD SERVICES
28606 Phillips Street

P.O. Box 968
Elkhart, IN 46515
(219) 264-3102

FOOD FIRST
398 60th Street
Oakland, CA 94618
(510) 654-4400

GRASSROOTS INTERNATIONAL
179 Boylston Street, 4th Floor
Boston, MA 02130
(617) 524-1400
e-mail: grassroots@igc.org

HUNGER RELIEF
American Friends Service
Committee
1501 Cherry Street
Philadelphia, PA 19102
(215) 241-7000

PHYSICIANS COMMITTEE FOR
RESPONSIBLE MEDICINE (PCRM)
5100 Wisconsin Avenue, NW,
Suite 404
Washington, DC 20016
(202) 686-2210
website: www.pcrm.org

OXFAM AMERICA
26 West Street
Boston, MA 02111
(617) 482-1211

SALVATION ARMY
World Service Office
615 Slaters Lane
Alexandria, VA 22313
(703) 684-5528

WHITE DOG CAFÉ
3420 Sansom Street
Philadelphia, PA 19104
(215) 386-9224
website: www.whitedog.com

Meditation

THE ASSOCIATION FOR RESEARCH
AND ENLIGHTENMENT, INC.
215 67th Street
Virginia Beach, VA 23451-2061
(800) 333-4499
e-mail: are@are-cayce.com
website: www.are-cayce.com

ANN WIGMORE FOUNDATION
P.O. Box 399
San Fidel, NM 87049
(505) 552-0595

BODY/MIND RESTORATION RETREAT,
ITHACA ZEN CENTER
56 Lieb Road
Spencer, NY 14883
(607) 272-0694 (phone/fax)
e-mail: bodymindr@aol.com

ELAT CHAYYIM: A CENTER FOR
HEALING AND RENEWAL
99 Mill Hood Road
Accord, NY 12404
(800) 398-2630 or (914) 626-
0157; fax (914) 626-2037
e-mail: elatchayyi@aol.com

ESALEN INSTITUTE
Highway 1
Big Sur, CA 93920-9616
(408) 667-3000
e-mail: catguy@esalen.org
website: www.eesalen.org

NEW LIFE HEALTH CENTER, INC.
12 Harris Avenue
Jamaica Plain, MA 02130
(617) 524-9551
e-mail: NHLCenter@aol.com
website: www.anewlife.com

NEW YORK OPEN CENTER, INC.
83 Spring Street
New York, NY 10012
(212) 219-2527
e-mail: box@opencenter.org
website: www.opencenter.org

OMEGA INSTITUTE FOR HOLISTIC
STUDIES
260 Lake Drive
Rhinebeck, NY 12572
(914) 266-4444
website: www.omega-inst.org

Natural Foods Companies

ARROWHEAD MILLS, INC.
P.O. Box 2059
Hereford, TX 79045
(806) 364-0730

CMC COMPANY
P.O. Box 322
Avalon, NJ 08202
(800) 262-2780

EDEN FOODS
701 Tecumseh Road
Clinton, Mich 49236
(888) 424-EDEN

GARDEN SPOT DISTRIBUTORS
438 White Oak Road

New Holland, PA 17557
(800) 829–5100

MAIL ORDER CATALOG
P.O. Box 180
Summertown, TN 338483
(800) 695-2241

MORI NU
2050 West 190th Street, No. 110
Torrance, CA 90504
(800) NOW-TOFU

NASOYA FOODS, INC.
Leominster, MA 01453
(800) 229-8638

WESTBRAE NATURAL FOODS
1065 East Walnut Street
Carson, CA 90746
(800) 769-6455

YVES VEGGIE CUISINE
1638 Derwent Way
Delta, BC, Canada V3M 6R9
(800) 667-9837; (604) 525-1345

Periodicals

AHIMSA
501 Old Harding Highway
Malaga, NJ 08328

ANIMALS' AGENDA
P.O. Box 2581
Baltimore, MD 21224

EAST-WEST JOURNAL
17 Station Street
P. O. Box 1200
Brookline, MA 02147

ENVIRONMENTAL ACTION
1525 New Hampshire Avenue, NW
Washington, DC 20036

MOTHER JONES
1663 Mission Street
San Francisco, CA 94103

NATURAL HEALTH
P.O. Box 1200
Brookline Village, MA 02147

ORION AFIELD
See The Orion Society

TURNING WHEEL
See Buddhist Peace Fellowship

Vegetarian Times
141 South Oak Park Avenue
P.O. Box 570
Oak Park, IL 60303
(800) 435-9610

VEGGIE LIFE
P. O. Box 57159
Boulder, CO 80322

Yoga/Meditation

INTEGRAL YOGA®
Satchidananda Ashram – Yogaville
Buckingham, VA 23921
(804) 969-1321

SELF-REALIZATION FELLOWSHIP
3880 San Rafael Avenue
Los Angeles, CA 90065
(323) 225-2471

BIBLIOGRAPHY

Ballentine, Martha. *Himalayan Mountain Cookery*. Honesdale, Penna.: Himalayan International Institute, 1976.

Barer-Stein, Thelma. *You Eat What You Are: A Study of Ethnic Food Traditions*. Toronto: Culture Concepts, 1991.

Barnard, M.D., Neal. *Food for Life: How the New Four Food Groups Can Save Your Life*. New York: Crown Publishers, 1993.

Bennett, Julienne, and Lubbermann, Mimi, eds. *Where the Heart Is: A Celebration of Home*. Novato, Calif.: New World Library, and Berkeley, Calif.: Wildcat Canyon Press, 1995.

Blue, Rabbi Lionel, and Rose, June. *A Taste of Heaven: Adventures in Food and Faith*. Springfield, Ill.: Templegate Publishers, 1977.

Brennan, Barbara. *Hands of Light: A Guide to Healing Through the Human Energy Field*. New York: Bantam Books, 1988.

Caldicott, M.D., Helen. *If You Love This Planet: A Plan to Heal the Earth*. New York: W. W. Norton & Co., 1992.

Chia, Mantak, and, Winn, Michael. *Taoist Secrets of Love: Cultivating Male Sexual Energy*. Santa Fe, N. M.: Aurora Press, 1984.

Chopra, M.D., Deepak. *Creating Health: Beyond Prevention, Toward Perfection*. Boston: Houghton Mifflin Co., 1987.

Collinge, William. *Subtle Energy: Awakening to the Unseen Forces in Our Lives*. New York: Warner Books, 1998.

Cook, John. *Diet and Your Religion: Advice for Living Better and Longer from the World's Great Religions*. Santa Barbara, Calif.: Woodbridge Press Publishing Co., 1976.

Copage, Eric V. *Kwanzaa: An African-American Celebration of Cooking and Culture*. New York: William Morrow and Co., Inc., 1991.

Crim, Keith, ed. *Abingdon Dictionary of Living Religions*. Nashville, Tenn.: Abingdon Press, 1981.

Cousens, M.D., Gabriel. *Conscious Eating*. Santa Rosa, Calif.: Vision Books International, 1992.

Devereux, Paul. *Earthmind: A Modern Adventure in Ancient Wisdom*. New York: Harper & Row Publishers, 1989.

Diamond, Harvey. *Your Heart, Your Planet*. Santa Monica, Calif.: Hay House, 1990.

Dossey, Larry. *Recovering the Soul*. New York: Bantam Books, 1989.

Douglas-Klotz, Neil. *Desert Wisdom: Sacred Middle Eastern Writings from the Goddess Through the Sufis*. San Francisco: HarperSanFrancisco, 1995.

Edidin, Ben M. *Jewish Customs and Ceremonies*. New York: Hebrew Publishing Co., 1941.

Edstrom, K.R.S. *Conquering Stress: The Skills You Need to Succeed in the Business World*. Hauppauge, N.Y.: Barron's Educational Series, 1993.

Eisenberg, M.D., David, with Wright, Thomas Lee. *Encounters with Qi: Exploring Chinese Medicine*. New York: W.W. Norton & Co., 1985.

Esquivel, Laura. *Like Water for Chocolate*. New York: Doubleday, 1992.

Findhorn Community. *The Findhorn Garden*. New York: Harper & Row Publishers, 1975.

Gaskell, G. A. *Dictionary of All Myths and Scriptures*. New York: Gramercy Books, 1981.

Gaster, Theodor H. *The Dead Sea Scriptures*. 3rd edition. New York: Anchor Books, 1976.

Gold, Peter. *Navajo and Tibetan Sacred Wisdom: The Circle of the Spirit*. Rochester, Vt.: Inner Traditions International, 1994.

Hahn, Thich Nhat. *The Miracle of Mindfulness*. Boston: Beacon Press, 1976.

Harman, Ph.D., Willis. *Global Mind Change: The Promise of the Last Years of the Twentieth Century*. Indianapolis, Ind.: Knowledge Systems, 1988.

Kabat-Zinn, Jon. *Wherever You Go There You Are: Mindfulness Meditation in Everyday Life*. New York: Hyperion, 1994.

———— *Full Catastrophe Living: Using the Wisdom of Your Body and Mind to Face Stress, Pain, and Illness*. New York: Delta/Dell (Bantam, Doubleday, Dell), 1990.

Kakuzo, Okakura. *The Book of Tea*. Rutland, Vt., and Tokyo: Charles E. Tuttle Co., 1974.

Kanai, Shigeru. *The Path to Self-Healing: Sotaiho*. Virginia Beach, Va.: Terra Bella Publishing, 1997.

Kass, Leon R M.D., *The Hungry Soul: Eating and the Perfecting of Our Nature*. New York: The Free Press, 1994.

Khan, Hazrat Inayat. *Philosophy, Psychology, Mysticism, and Aphorisms*. The Sufi Message of Hazrat Inayat Khan, vol. 2. London: Barrie and Rockliff, 1964.

Kelly, Marcia and Jack. *One Hundred Graces*. New York: Bell Tower/Harmony/Crown, 1992.

Klaper, M.D., Michael. *Vegan Nutrition, Pure and Simple*. Maui, Hi: Gentle World Publishing, 1987.

Kushi, Aveline, and Esko, Wendy. *The Changing Seasons Macrobiotic Cookbook*. Wayne, N.J.: Avery Publishing Group, 1985.

Lad, Vasant. *Ayurveda: The Science of Self-Healing*. Santa Fe, N.M.: Lotus Press, 1984.

Lindfield, Michael. *The Dance of Change: An Eco-Spiritual Approach to Transformation*. London: Arkana Paperbacks, 1986.

Lemkow, Anna F. *The Wholeness Principle: Dynamics of Unity Within Science, Religion, and Society*. Wheaton, Ill.: The Theosophical Publishing House, 1990.

Levin, Cecile Tovah. *Cooking for Regeneration: Macrobiotic Relief from Cancer, AIDS, and Degenerative Disease*. Tokyo and New York: Japan Publications, 1988.

Linn, Denise. *Sacred Space: Clearing and Enhancing the Energy of Your Home*. New York: Ballantine Books, 1995.

Lliteras, D. S. *The Thieves of Golgotha*. Charlottesville, Va.: Hampton Roads Publishing Co., 1998.

McDougall, M.D., John A., and McDougall, Mary A. *The McDougall Plan*. Piscataway, N.J.: New Century Publishers, 1983.

Morningstar, Amadea, with Desai, Urmila. *The Ayurvedic Cookbook*. Wilmot, Wisc.: Lotus Press, 1990.

Nigosian, Solomon. *Judaism: The Way of Holiness*. London: The Aquarian Press, 1987.

Ohsawa, George. *Essential Ohsawa: From Food to Health, Happiness to Freedom*. Garden City Park, N.Y.: Avery Publishing Group, 1994.

Ornish, M.D., Dean. *Dr. Dean Ornish's Program for Reversing Heart Disease*. New York: Ballantine Books, 1996.

———. *Eat More, Weigh Less*. New York: HarperCollins Publishers, 1993.

Panati, Charles. *Sacred Origins of Profound Things*. New York: Penguin/Arkana, 1996.

Pickarski, Ron. *Eco-Cuisine: An Ecological Approach to Gourmet Vegetarian Cooking*. Berkeley, Calif.: Ten Speed Press, 1995.

———. *Friendly Foods*. Berkeley, Calif.: Ten Speed Press, 1991.

Powers, John. *Introduction to Tibetan Buddhism*. Ithaca, N. Y.: Snow Lion Publications, 1995.

Robbins, John. *Diet for a New America: How Your Food Choices Affect Your Health, Happiness, and the Future of Life on Earth*. Walpole, N.H.: Stillpoint Publishing, 1987.

———. *May All Be Fed: Diet for a New World*. New York: William Morrow and Co., Inc., 1992.

Robertson, Robin. *The Soy Gourmet: Improve Your Health the Natural Way with 75 Delicious Recipes*. New York: Penguin/Plume, 1998.

Rossbach, Sarah. *Feng Shui: The Chinese Art of Placement*. New York: Penguin/Arkana, 1983.

Sams, Jamie. *Earth Medicine: Ancestors' Ways of Harmony for Many Moons*. San Francisco: HarperSanFrancisco, 1994.

Satchidananda, Sri Swami. *The Golden Present*. Buckingham, Va.: Integral Yoga Publications, 1992.

Siegel, M.D., Bernie S. *Love, Medicine, and Miracles*. New York: Harper & Row Publishers, 1986.

Smith, Huston. *The Religions of Man*. New York: Harper & Row Publishers, 1958.

Strassfeld, Michael. *The Jewish Holidays: A Guide and Commentary*. New York: Harper & Row Publishers, 1985.

Szekely, Edmond Bordeaux. *The Essene Gospel of Peace, Book One*. Matsqui, B.C., Canada: International Biogenic Society, 1981.

Telushkin, Rabbi Joseph. *Jewish Wisdom: Ethical, Spiritual, and Historical Lessons from the Great Works and Thinkers*. New York: William Morrow and Co., Inc., 1994.

Tobias, Michael, and Cowan, Georgianne, eds. *The Soul of Nature: Visions of a Living Earth*. New York: The Continuum Publishing Co., 1994.

Trungpa, Chögyam. *The Myth of Freedom and the Way of Meditation*. Berkeley, Calif., and London: Shambhala Publications, 1976.

Visser, Margaret. *The Rituals of Dinner*. New York: Penguin Books, 1991.

Weil, M.D., Andrew. *Spontaneous Healing*. New York: Alfred. A. Knopf, 1995.

———— *Natural Health, Natural Medicine: A Comprehensive Manual for Wellness and Self-Care*. Boston: Houghton Mifflin Co., 1990.

Williams, William E. *Unbounded Light: The Inward Journey*. York Beach, Me.: Nicholas-Hays, 1992.

Wright, Machaelle Small. *Behaving As If the God in All Life Mattered*. Warrenton, Va.: Perelandra, Ltd., 1997.

Yoneda, Soei. *The Heart of Zen Cuisine*. New York: Kodansha International Ltd., 1987.

Zaleski, Philip, and Kaufman, Paul. *Gifts of the Spirit: Living the Wisdom of the Great Religious Traditions*. New York: HarperCollins Publishers, 1998.

INDEX